The Personals

The Personals

The human stories behind the small ads

Brian O'Connell

HarperCollins*Publishers*

In order to protect privacy, some names, identifying characteristics, dialogue and details have been changed or reconstructed.

HarperCollins*Publishers*
1 London Bridge Street
London SE1 9GF

www.harpercollins.co.uk

First published by HarperCollins*Publishers* 2019

3 5 7 9 10 8 6 4

Text © Brian O'Connell 2019
Illustrations © Micaela Alcaino 2019

Brian O'Connell asserts the moral right to be identified as the author of this work

A catalogue record of this book is available from the British Library

ISBN 978-0-00-832134-5

Printed and bound in Great Britain by
CPI Group (UK) Ltd, Croydon, CR0 4YY

All rights reserved. No part of this publication may be reproduced, stored in a retrieval system, or transmitted, in any form or by any means, electronic, mechanical, photocopying, recording or otherwise, without the prior written permission of the publishers.

MIX
Paper from
responsible sources
FSC™ C007454

This book is produced from independently certified FSC™ paper to ensure responsible forest management

For more information visit: www.harpercollins.co.uk/green

'Just for a second, I thought I lost myself,
And I watched my body falling,
And all the colours look brighter now.'

Brian Carey, RIP

CONTENTS

Introduction   1

PART ONE: LOVE AND LOSS

When East Meets West   11
A Ringless Marriage   21
A Dress for the (Middle) Ages   31
A Chance Encounter of a Shocking Kind   34
A Long Engagement   40
Addicted to Love?   47
A Marriage Worth Waiting For   56

PART TWO: EQUIPPED FOR LIFE

The Car That's Bulletproof   67
For Your Eyes Only   70
Running Up That Hill   76

PART THREE: PETS' CORNER

A Monkey Is for Life – Not Just for Christmas	91
Finding Shangri-La	93
Making It Pig in Hollywood	104

PART FOUR: ARTICLES OF WAR

Married to the Past	113
'Grow Wheat – The Crop That Pays'	117
Zen and the Art of Phone Box Maintenance	123
Engineering a Step Back in Time	130
The Weight of History	136

PART FIVE: SENTIMENTAL VALUE

Rekindling a One in a Million Chance	153
Remains of a Detached Day	159
Giving a Doll's House a Home	166

PART SIX: COLLECTORS

'We Are Collectors ... and We Will Die as Collectors'	175
Signing the Past Away	183

PART SEVEN: LOST CAUSES?

Being Frank	195
Building a Bigger Shrine	201

PART EIGHT: THIS MORTAL COIL

Meeting a Man About a Hearse	209
Plotting a Way Out of Grief	221

PART NINE: SIGNS OF THE TIMES

Nursing Hidden Desires	231
Cut-Price Counselling	243
The Homeless Hotel	256
Making Study Pay	266
Acknowledgements	275

INTRODUCTION

The story goes that Ernest Hemingway and a few of his literary pals were knocking about the Algonquin Hotel in New York one night in the 1920s, before they had the joys of social media to help them avoid conversation, and they began challenging each other to write a novel using just six words. Cutting a long story short, Hemingway is said to have won hands down with the words: 'For Sale: Baby Shoes, Never Worn.'

He's reputed to have said that those six words were the best he ever wrote. They are loaded with life experience, love, loss, death and hope perhaps; a six-word portal into lived experience that Dorothy Parker or William Carlos Williams might have been proud of. The only problem is, while this sounds a plausible story that has been handed down over decades as literary fact, it probably never happened – or if it did happen, it almost certainly predated Hemingway and his bohemian clique. An essay about a similar short story by William R. Kane appeared in 1917 and a newspaper

The Personals

column by R. K. Moulton in 1921 pointed to an advert he had seen: 'Baby Carriage for Sale: Never Used' and informed his readers that it embodied the plot of a story. The Hemingway anecdote probably evolved over time, as a literary agent more or less admitted decades later when he said that he had first heard the story from a newspaper syndicator in the mid-1970s, more than a decade after Hemingway had died.

The point is that classified ads have long held fascination as a rich source of human experience and stories. When starting out in journalism in local media, I remember staring out of the window on a dreary Tuesday morning, stuck for story ideas for that morning's pitching session. I shared my frustration with an older editor, who told me to try the small ads. So I did, and I have returned to them again and again in the two decades since as a source of stories.

In an era of PR handlers and press releases, of government advertising camouflaged as journalism, and carefully chosen interviewees who are sometimes over-coached and underwhelming, the world of classified ads, both online and in print, offers an unfiltered window into society.

I've spent almost two decades in journalism, and something interesting has happened in that time. People have never put as much of themselves out there as they do today, whether through social or digital media, or by sharing their stories or 'opening up' in

Introduction

more traditional media. There have never been so many filters or gatekeepers trying to shape those narratives. Sometimes an interviewee may have shared their story online, had a media training workshop, or may already possess a 'them and us' mentality about journalists and the media in general before I even get to speak to them. Some of that mistrust is warranted, and very healthy of course, but there's also cynicism in a lot of encounters, and many more competing agendas than previously when I sit across from someone and press record.

When using Instagram, Snapchat, Facebook live, video and audio messaging we are all much more aware of how we project ourselves than ever before. As a result, people often display a caginess and deep self-awareness of how they conduct themselves during an interview. One contradiction I've come across is that the more people are willing to expose of their lives online, the less personal and intimate they may want to be in one-to-one encounters. Authenticity can become a casualty, chance encounters become less likely and conversations without agendas are at a premium.

Hopefully, because of all that, you can see why personal ads – and the people and lives and secrets and stories and heartbreak and quirkiness that sometimes lie behind them – are so appealing to this forty-something and somewhat sentimental hack, and why I thought they would work well collected in a book. The ads allow me to move away from the managed

The Personals

world of spin doctors and carefully planned media campaigns to a less self-conscious world – one that I think is at times more authentic.

Of course, part of this book is about items for sale, but that section is also about the off-piste moments when an ad for a ring turns into a discussion about dementia, or a poster for sale reveals the struggles of independent shops in rural Ireland. These ads also show how letting go of an item becomes a lesson in how to own your grief, or how living with and then discarding addiction can paradoxically set you free. Classified ads brought me into people's lives for no other reason than the fact that they let me in. There were no PR agencies, no communication strategies, no media advisers and no campaigns wrapped tightly around case studies. As they say on *Judge Judy*, the stories are real, the people are real!

On a basic level, I'm also drawn to these ads because they throw up some humdingers of stories. The excitement for me, and I hope for you reading this, is going from a few lines of text to the trenches of the First World War, or getting an insight into the complexities of a relationship break-up, or the obsessive mind of a fixated collector – or simply capturing a time or a story or an experience that would otherwise not be documented.

When I was about halfway through researching this book, my wife peered into my office and saw me sitting

Introduction

with my feet on the desk, steaming cup of tea in hand, scrolling through a list of 'never worn' wedding dresses for sale. The slightly worrying thing is that she didn't bat an eyelid. My obsession with classified ads is really an obsession with people's lives and stories – the ads are just a doorway through which I stick my head.

There was a time not long ago when I sourced most of these stories solely from ads in print media – places such as the *Irish Farmer's Journal*, *Ireland's Own*, *The Echo* and many broadsheets had extensive classified sections, as well as personal pages. The majority of these ads have migrated online, as sites such as Craigslist and later Adverts, Gumtree and DoneDeal made it much easier to buy and sell in the digital era. And so I have followed suit.

By collating a selection of recent adverts and some I have captured over the last few years, I want to take you down lanes and into homes, into hearts and cluttered minds and tell stories that would not otherwise be told. In all except maybe half a dozen of these stories, I have met the people behind the ads in person, usually travelling to their homes or meeting them in a car or cafe nearby. When that wasn't possible, or the poster did not want to meet, we spoke at length on the phone or through email.

What draws me into these ads are the personal stories – the reasons for a break-up, how a child collector became an adult one or why someone feels the need to sell a treasured ring that has come to represent something tainted or tragic.

Through the years there have been some important ads that have signalled significant societal change. These were the ads in the early part of the twentieth century looking for 'good Catholic homes' for the children of 'fallen women' for example, or the aged bachelor farmers looking for girls in their late teens to become 'life partners', or those looking for domestic servants, or the emigrants in Australia trying to reconnect with family many decades later. You could write a whole social history on the classified ads of past decades.

Two books worth reading on this are *Strange Red Cow*, Sarah Bader's fascinating trawl through the vintage classified ads of US publications, and *Classified* by H. G. Cocks, an interesting take on how sexuality and society evolved in Britain, again through the prism of the small ads. In his book, Cocks traces the rise of personal ads to respectability, from one of the first ecclesiastical style ads in the fifteenth century through the invention of modern newspapers in the mid-seventeenth century right up to today. One of his central points is that the internet today 'merely accelerates processes which, when people had to rely on print and the postal service, just took longer to achieve.' Cocks makes a compelling argument that the small ad was a 'symbol of everything that was both exciting and dangerous about modern sexuality' and

Introduction

that the classifieds have been a gateway to all sorts of delights and dangers ever since their invention, showing how ordinary people grappled with love, sex, marriage, friendship and commerce through recent centuries.

All the stories in this book are quite recent and attempt to document snapshots of life in Ireland today. There are also stories and ads which I hope bring history to life – such as the military medals and memorabilia for sale, the nineteenth-century hearse, the impact of mother and baby homes or the frayed match programme for a long forgotten All-Ireland final.

I've divided the book into parts and the timeline roughly spans the period from 2012 to the present. In several of the stories, you'll notice that I haven't given the name of the person posting the ad and don't identify where they're located, or I've used a pseudonym. This is at their request and I was happy to proceed on the basis that no one was identified, especially with some of the more sensitive ads. I don't think this detracts from the account of their experiences.

The way I sourced the material was simple. Most weeks I scoured the small ads in places such as the *Evening Echo* (since renamed *The Echo*) or online on DoneDeal. I was looking for hints that there was a story or a life experience worth hearing hidden behind the few lines of text on page or screen.

When I thought an ad had potential I would text the poster, explain that I was interested in the story

The Personals

behind it and ask whether they would take a call. Some thought I was part of an elaborate scam to fiddle them out of their item for sale, while others, particularly those recently bereaved, were very happy to sit and talk about their life experiences.

I'm very grateful to everyone who shared their stories and let me into their homes, or met me in hotels, cafes or parked cars, or took a phone call and spilled their heart out and shared with me intimate details of their life. There was really nothing in it for them; by the time this book is published most of their ads will have long since expired, so it was hugely refreshing to be able to talk to people simply because they wanted to share some of their story with me.

While the ad is a signpost, it's ultimately the people who drew me in, and the adage that everyone has a story. The privilege for me is in contacting a stranger and shortly afterwards sharing some of the more intimate moments of their life, with no agenda or preconditions. Throughout this process the joy was in finding unexpected twists and turns, lessons learned and the life experiences gained, all trapped iceberg-like beneath a few lines of classified text on a page or screen. Those kinds of discoveries are what brought me back again and again to these stories.

Some people do Sudoku, others binge on box sets; I trawl the classified ads ...

Part One
LOVE AND LOSS

WHEN EAST MEETS WEST

> **Beautiful wedding and engagement ring for sale. €3,000 or nearest offer.** *DoneDeal, June 2018*

Weeds are growing up through the barriers at the edge of the estate I'm driving through, as Google Maps and I have one of our many disagreements and I circle round at least half a dozen times.

The gravel-filled fields beyond those barriers were once called 'Phase 2' on a glossy Celtic Tiger era brochure, probably launched in a penthouse with a rugby player and canapés. Now the scabby site adjacent remains a stubborn scar on the landscape, a reminder that we lost control and that this estate was over-hyped and over-extended until the building came to an abrupt end.

I'm in one of the attractive, three-bedroomed, semi-detached houses which could easily have been

The Personals

the show house. Large candles are lit around the fireplace and there's one of those evocative black and white coastal prints on the wall. Despite the welcome, it has been made clear to me that I will have to grant anonymity to the seller, because the events which led to the rings being put up for sale were relatively recent and raw. Apart from that precondition, she really wanted to tell her story and had seemed warm and friendly on the phone.

She is a fortysomething woman, and in her sitting room there are clues that she is well travelled – an African mask here, an Asian figurine there. I'm not sure that it's a house that has seen many four a.m. Christy Moore singalongs; everything seems particularly placed, and because we meet just as she's come in from work, I assume that the house always looks this gleaming and wasn't scrubbed for my sake. I also guess that no small children live here – the lighted candles and open bowls of potpourri give this away.

We take a seat on the couch and I can see she's a little nervous, but also quite open, and in her hand, she flips the lid of a ring box open and closed while we make small talk and I compliment her on the interior. I watch as each flick open reveals glistening stones, while each movement shut smothers the sparkly diamonds in darkness. She tells me that her rings have been in this box since last year and pauses, presumably waiting for me to ask what happened. I hold off as I often do in these encounters. Sometimes the longer you hold off talking about the elephant in the room the louder the elephant will demand to be heard. Also, we're having tea and the biscuits are really nice.

By way of easing into the story, I ask her to describe the rings to me, which saves me the embarrassment of discussing something I know zilch about. 'The engagement ring is a solitaire ring and it has encrusted diamonds halfway on each shoulder,' she explains, thinking about, and then resisting the urge, to put it on her finger. 'The wedding ring would have the same type of encrusted diamonds. So, this is a band of diamonds and they have the same set on the side. They are stunning rings. I think in total it's one carat. I initially picked the diamonds and I got them in Dubai and the company that were making them for me called me up to say they had sourced a nicer-quality diamond, and they were looking for permission to put it in. So, it was crafted with great care and consideration and there's no inscription on them.'

The rings, the box, the inlay cards and the lack of inscription all make it look as if they've just come off the shelf from a high-street jeweller. Have they ever actually been on her finger, I ask? 'Yes, they went on my finger in December 2015 and they came off in September 2017. So just under two years. Do you want to know the story?'

The Personals

As we continued to chat over tea and Club Milks, it became clear that while parts of this story were about lost love (or perhaps false love), another part was about the pressure to conform. More accurately, it's about the social anxiety that builds when you get to your late thirties, see your friends marry and partner up one by one, and feel that part of society has its sights fixed on you and that some judge you by your singleness. In reality of course, those who have partnered up and are dealing with early morning Peppa Pig breakfasts are probably so preoccupied with lack of sleep and reducing their mortgage repayments that they barely notice anything except their expanding midriffs and greying hairs.

That insight into single life will come later; for now I ask my host if she would like to tell me how she fell in love. 'Well, I married a non-EU national, someone from the Middle East, in Lebanon in December 2015,' she explains, in a voice that's not so much bitter as rueful. 'We had known each other a year and a half at

that stage. What attracted me to him was his drive and his commitment to working with young people. I share the same values. He proposed to me and of course I said yes to this handsome man.'

And for the first time the nerves are gone and she's smiling as she recounts their early courtship. Had she any hesitation at the time, I ask? 'In my naivety, no,' she says. 'I had considered motivations briefly; why he would ask someone to marry so quickly, but I would have thought maybe he loved me. I didn't really question that. I should have.'

After they married, she returned home in late 2015, and after Christmas that year applied for his spousal visa so he could come to Ireland. This application turned into a lengthy and intrusive process during which their relationship needed to be verified, requiring testimony from family and friends that it was a legitimate marriage.

All her family were happy to give their testimony, and all were convinced this relationship was for real. In total, the process cost €4,000. This should have been the starting point for a wonderful life together in Ireland. Instead, it became the point at which their short marriage came unstuck and she felt the gaze of partnered society even more acutely. 'His visa was refused in August 2017,' she says. 'And the day after I told him it had been refused, he told me he was marrying someone else. Just like that.'

The Personals

Her voice fills with emotion as she tells me this, as when someone recalls a recent bereavement. Two weeks after that phone call she was devastated when it was confirmed that her husband had in fact married someone else. While their relationship had been long distance, he had been to Ireland for a visit, and she had been to his country several times, and they spoke on the phone every day. But a fortnight after she had told him of the visa refusal, her husband's new wife sent her a screenshot of their marriage certificate. Talk about moving on quickly ...

It's a difficult question, but I ask her whether she thinks his second marriage was prompted by the visa refusal. After a long pause, she looks at me with reddening eyes and says: 'Yeah. I think it was just a matter of what will he do next to make life comfortable for himself? I think he was able to draw a line under it very quickly and move on to his next plan. He denied it for a while. His family confirmed he had got married again, and for a while I was bargaining with him, saying, "It is OK; you can remain married to her and remain married to me as well," – he can have four wives after all, because of his culture.'

Our conversation was taking place 11 months after the break-up and while the wound is still not fully healed, she has moved on significantly. She shakes her head when she tells me about her attempts to bargain with him, and how she considered allowing her husband to have another wife in another country. She recognises this as a sign of her desperation to keep him and their marriage, whatever the cost. It's totally understandable, I tell her – she'd told all her friends and family, had the big day, made life plans with someone and then, bang, it was all pulled from under her.

'It was an enormous shock. I was definitely not able to eat for about three weeks,' she says. 'I couldn't even talk about it, to be honest. There was a lot of shame because I should have known better. You read these things in magazines and you see these things on TV shows. And you are saying to yourself, that would never happen to me, how stupid could that person be? But, it's not until you experience it and are drawn and pulled into it, in what appears to be a meaningful relationship. And then you have utter shame around falling for it. But it happens …'

'Yes, it happens,' I say reassuringly. Her vulnerability is clear, and while I can see she has thought long and hard about this whole episode, and has probably spent many nights looking at those log-sized candles flickering and filling the empty space on the couch beside her, the grief has not gone away; she has just learned to adapt to it most of the time.

What's keeping her anchored to the sailed ship that was her marriage is the fact that she cannot legally divorce her husband, despite the fact that he is living with another woman in another country. 'I'm not able to divorce him from here,' she affirms. 'I don't want to go over there and get divorced. But I have made enquiries and the only choice I have is to hire a solicitor in his country to do the divorce or else go back to the mosque so he would have to grant it. I was advised not to go ...'

So, while she figures out how to remove herself from the marriage, she is faced with legal bills for the failed visa application, not to mention the costs associated with the wedding, most of which she has borne. The engagement and wedding rings were bought in Dubai. In total they cost €5,000, the majority of which she paid herself. She will sell them for €3,000. 'They are stunning rings,' she adds. 'When they were on my hand, everyone would stop and pick them up and look at the weight of them and remark how stunning they were. You won't get them on anyone else in Ireland.'

There's obviously both an emotional and financial catharsis in getting rid of the rings as quickly as she can now. Anyone who has ever been in a failed relationship will tell you it has an impact long after the last tears have been shed. But in a situation like this, when there was no advance warning, and when one party feels they were duped into love, that impact is all the more magnified. 'I am getting there now but immediately afterwards you do question what men say. You analyse them more now and I guess I've to be very careful I don't bring this into a new relationship,' she says candidly.

I tell her that her openness and insight and her inherent humanity (which she says is often interpreted as naivety) should not have to become a casualty of this. These are the things I tell her that will paradoxically give her the best chance of falling in love again. There is something likeable about my interviewee. She has warmth and oozes care, compassion and decency. I imagine she is the kind of person who sees a news bulletin about famine in Yemen or drought in Kenya and hits the donate button there and then. But I wonder how much the failed marriage has changed her; how much it has made her less receptive to love. 'I would be more self-aware now,' she says. 'I know I was a little bit naive. But I would prefer this way than to be cynical. I would prefer to be able to fall in love than to always query and question. I think that's a lonely life. I won't be too cynical about it. I mean, there wasn't ever a question of whether I loved him or not.'

Before I leave she carefully puts the rings back in their boxes, and as she's doing so, I ask what is the biggest lesson she's learned from the whole experience. 'I think that it can happen anyone and I think, well, you can beat yourself up about it but I think you can in the future say to yourself, you need to step back from a situation and try to look at it from different perspec-

The Personals

tives. Some of my friends would have said, you know, are you sure about this? Without overtly coming out and saying I was being duped. I said, of course I'm sure; he loves me, he tells me it. Those same friends have never come back and said we told you so. If you're hurt to that extent, then you have to reflect on what you have done, what would I have done differently – am I that vulnerable, naive and gullible? You ask yourself all those questions. You question yourself if a man says to you, "You look lovely." I hate that it has changed me that way, but it's to be expected, I suppose.'

Does she ever wear the rings now? 'No. Not any more. They're not mine now. I hope they go on someone's finger that will have many years of happy marriage.'

We finish our tea. I tell her that I hope she's talking to people about how she feels, and she says she has some very close friends and they share. She's determined not to allow the whole experience to inhibit her or in any way reduce her chances of finding 'the one'.

Somehow, I think she's going to be OK and I leave thinking that selling the rings is the manifestation of a need to start again, of choosing deliberately to put what were once symbols of the future firmly into the past.

A RINGLESS MARRIAGE

> **Vintage wedding and engagement ring for sale; €2,000 or nearest offer. Comes with valuation.** *DoneDeal, July 2018*

I'm early and have parked outside a house in the west of Ireland. I'm sitting in my car waiting for the owner of the above rings to arrive home. Someone is knocking on my car window and wants to lead me into the house. As I follow, a large Alsatian appears and eyes me from inside the open front door. Just then a Land Rover pulls into the drive and a woman gets out, brushes past me and quickly closes the door before the Alsatian bolts. 'Sorry about that,' she says, before adding casually, 'That dog bites.' She half chides the man who let the dog out, before asking if I want tea or coffee and clearing a space at the kitchen table for us to sit.

I notice that the man is quite self-conscious and I also notice that she's overseeing his tea making, or at

The Personals

least subtly checking each step while trying not to make it obvious that she is doing so. The kitchen is cluttered – managed clutter, I'd call it – and even though the house is on a main road in a village, outside are a collection of sheds and outbuildings, bales of hay and fields. I'm guessing that they grew up on farms, and this is their way of keeping one foot in the fields, living on the side of a busy road, yet constructing a mini farmyard out back.

There's a nervousness in the room and some tension. I don't sense that it's caused by me or my microphone. I think it's more the fact that their space is now shared with someone else and they're very conscious of that. As cups of coffee are served the man gets closer to me without saying anything, as if he is afraid to say the wrong thing. And then I notice the box on the windowsill behind the sink. Every day of the month has a little window and some are open, advent calendar like, while others are unopened. Inside are red and white pills, and the day and date is printed on each little portal.

Something clicks, and I'm taken back to an interview I'd done years earlier beside a mountain in Tipperary, with a man and his mother, who was in the final stages of dementia. She kept pleading with me to take her away because she believed he was poisoning her. He wasn't, of course. In reality he was keeping her alive, and had sacrificed much of his own life to ensure his mother could stay in her own home as long as possible. Her illness meant that she took her anger and frustration out on him every day. She kept saying to me over and over, pointing to imaginary marks on her body: 'Look what he did to me ... *look*.' And there they lived, together and alone at the foot of a mountain; mother and adult son entwined in their love and false hate, their reality and their fiction. Long after I'd driven away from the house they were still with me. They are in my mind now in this half farmhouse, where two adults are reframing their relationship, forgotten fragment by forgotten fragment.

The man's wife tells me that his dementia and diagnosis of Alzheimer's has been a relatively recent discovery, or more accurately, that she didn't know her husband had been diagnosed until recently. 'I felt there was something going on,' she says. 'He was short-tempered and not totally focused on certain chores we would share. He wouldn't do them, or he would forget where the keys were. Those things didn't come in one day – it was over a period of a week. The biggest thing that made me go to the doctor with him was the fact that he wasn't concerned about how he was dressed. He would forget things. More and more he would forget where keys were or that he put milk in the fridge without using it; silly little things really.'

Throughout these changes her husband didn't seem particularly bothered, she says. When he got frustrated,

The Personals

he would lose his temper a little and it could be over the smallest of things. For example, if she asked him if he'd put the kettle on and make coffee, he might get a little hot-tempered and react by saying he was always doing it. She believes now that he has had dementia since 2016, and that Alzheimer's developed after that. He is aware that he has Alzheimer's, but doesn't accept that the change in his life is due to the condition. There should be a lot more help and support for families like theirs, she says, and sometimes she feels alone and abandoned by state services. There are practical things that need to be done, such as signing the house over to their children, which he is reluctant to do.

'He is changing into someone else,' she says. 'I could put my arms around him today and say, "I love you". I could whisper in his ear that we had a great life and sometimes his response will be more measured. He might agree and say, "Remind me again how many years we are together?" But I could do the same thing later in the day, especially in bed, and he will push me away and say, "Stop that now, I have to sleep." It's hard to know how he will react sometimes.'

She says he can be very curt and sharp with her, and often if she is upset or crying he won't stop what he's doing to ask how she is and will simply walk by, oblivious to her feelings. She tries to continue to treat him as normally as she can, especially in front of other people. It would hurt him if she treated him any

A Ringless Marriage

differently. Increasingly, she has been taking him with her when she has to leave the house. This is partly because it's good for him to get out and about and not isolate himself, but also, at least when he is with her she knows he is safe and won't wander down the road or leave the door open.

Of course she worries about the future, and she worries too about how much longer she will be able to manage the situation. She's done a lot of research into the condition and she believes that often it follows the personality and character of the person living with it. 'In general terms, if the person is a quiet gentle partner and takes things in their stride and is easy-going, then often that is how it will be for them,' she says. 'My husband has always been active and forthright, like me, and he could lose his temper on certain things, so his illness is a manifestation of that.'

She's aware that he's in the early stages of the illness. The medication available can slow it down, and while it does have an impact, she wishes she had known about her husband's diagnosis sooner. Maybe he forgot to tell her, or a letter from his consultant might have been mislaid. Either way, she feels huge guilt for having arguments with him about forgetting certain things, when all along he had been given the dementia diagnosis and she didn't know about it.

'He was the kind of man that if anything in the house needed mending, he was on top of it,' she says.

The Personals

'Now, if a radiator leaks, he will say, "I will fix it" and often it will be leaking even more afterwards. If I say anything, he will blame me for it and tell me to do it myself. I'm telling you all this because it's not easy and there are significant challenges, and it's heart-breaking to see someone you love change so much.'

As he tidied up she watched and tried not to make it obvious that she was overseeing what he was doing. We moved to the sitting room, where she produced a velvet pouch and began taking out rings. She was very deliberate in how she handled them, having taken them from an old shoebox which also contained several letters and some other items of jewellery. To my surprise, it turns out that the rings didn't belong to her. 'They're my late mother's rings,' she says. 'And she never wore them.'

The box contained two rings. One was an engagement ring made of 18 carat white gold. To my untrained eye it looked more like yellow gold, but most people would describe it simply as a diamond cluster ring. The wedding ring was also 18 carats, again white gold, and it was more modest than the engagement ring. Both came with their certificates and valuation forms. While she's connected to them emotionally, I don't get the sense that they are treasured deeply. There's something in the way she holds them in her hand – the casualness perhaps, or the fact that there's a firm-handedness in her movements with

A Ringless Marriage

the rings. When I suggest this, she corrects me. 'They do mean an awful lot to me,' she says, 'but I can't keep them because I think they are better off on somebody's finger, rather than just shutting them away in a safe.'

When she told me that they had been her mother's and never worn, of course I thought of all sorts of heart-breaking reasons why. But she tells me that her mother had gone ahead with the marriage. In fact, it had been her second marriage. And the reason she hadn't worn the rings was fairly simple – she had still been in love with her first husband. How had her second husband responded to that? 'He respected it. You see, my parents loved each other very much, but they couldn't live together. The marriage was very difficult when they were living together but they became best of friends after they divorced.'

We're talking here about the mid-1970s, when the seller's mother had remarried. At that stage, she had been separated from her first husband for about six years. Sadly, she passed away some years ago in a nursing home in England, while the seller's father moved to Eastern Europe, where he also remarried. While they were both alive, they had kept in touch. And the last time her mother and father actually met each other? 'It was at my brother's funeral,' she tells me. 'He had a heart attack and died suddenly. My father came home and he stayed alongside my mother at the funeral, sitting really close beside her. It was clear the connection was still there. I think they both had the same type of character and personality – the same type of short fuse.'

Telling me the story of her parents' divorce and their subsequent friendliness towards each other, she says she doesn't want to over-romanticise it. It's not just the story of two people thrown together and then pulled apart and yet still there for each other at the end. Her parents had separated after a period of time when the arguments between them became worse as their children moved through their teenage years. She doesn't want to go into it too much, but those years left their mark and did have an impact on her in later years. Luckily, when her mother remarried, her daughter always got on very well with her stepfather. She describes him as a fantastic man, and totally in love with her mother.

'He was a gentleman. A small man. Very, very polite and very gentle,' she says. 'He loved my mother so much. He would do anything for her. When she started getting ill, he gave up his job and he waited on her hand and foot. He would buy her anything, take her wherever she wanted to go. And when she had to go to a nursing home, he gave up work and went and sat with her every single day. He absolutely idolised her.'

When the man had given her mother the engagement and wedding rings now on the table in front of

A Ringless Marriage

me, what did she do with them if she didn't wear them? 'She had a chain,' her daughter tells me, 'which I have, and she put the two rings on a silver chain and put it around her neck. And she went through the rest of her life with no rings on her fingers. I also have her first wedding rings. These ones are too valuable to be just left in a safe. To me these two rings are beautiful but I don't feel the same connection with them as her first wedding rings. I idolised my stepfather but he has also given me the right and the blessing to sell them.'

The rings are now for sale for €2,000. She would be thrilled to get €1,500 for them and to know that they have been given a new lease of life. I tell her I admire her for putting them up for sale. Her mother had made a defiant stance in not wearing them and she is now making another by selling them. Why be weighed down by the past? If she does succeed in selling them, the money is already accounted for, she tells me. 'I will buy my mother a little plaque which has a mother's verse on it and I want to put it on her grave from her children.'

So far she's had a few offers but won't let the rings go for much below the asking price. I ask her finally whether she'd ever talked to her parents about the years she lived with them when they were having difficulties in their marriage. 'I did,' she tells me, 'I spoke to my father. I didn't get a chance to speak to my mother. He always said he would keep a special place

The Personals

in his heart for my mother and he respected her and he said it was such a pity they could not live together. He is 86 years old now and lives in a different country, but he always advised me to never go to bed on a row.'

She keeps this in mind, even with the added difficulty of caring for her husband during his illness. The years ahead will be uncertain, so now feels the right time to break with the past, and move on. She's hoping for the right buyer and will be slow to let the rings go to a dealer or speculator. 'Even though my mother never wore these rings, there is a lot of happiness in them,' she tells me. 'They just need to find a home now.'

A DRESS FOR THE (MIDDLE) AGES

For sale: beautiful medieval-style wedding dress. Never worn. *Evening Echo, 2014*

Jane lives in a small two-up, two-down in Cork city with her husband and two cats. She studied history at university but a series of illnesses meant that she had to give up her work as a part-time tutor. Two days a week she now works from home – a job, coincidentally, that she found through the classifieds. Jane always wanted a traditional church wedding, but her fiancé wanted something less conventional and more 'out there'. They compromised and decided on a medieval-themed wedding in a church. Jane ordered her dress, a medieval satin designer gown, from a designer in the United States.

So far so good, but as the day of the wedding grew nearer, the pressure of getting married got to the couple. Ireland was still clawing its way out of recession and the lack of credit on offer from their bank meant they were worried about getting into more debt. Her fiancé had to travel long distances for work so they spent more and more time apart. After weeks of discussion the wedding was postponed.

As you can imagine, the couple and both their families were devastated. 'My dress was made of cream velvet with large bell sleeves and a criss-cross design in the front and back,' Jane explains. 'We had it all planned and everything and for one reason and another it didn't take place and we put off the wedding for a while.'

Thankfully, this story does have a happy ending and the couple ended up having a medieval blessing on Cape Clear Island in summer 2013. Jane wore a more

A Dress for the (Middle) Ages

casual medieval dress for the occasion and her husband dressed as a knight. He wore four patches of colours and a long gown and both arrived at the ceremony carrying large swords. The blessing came from an old Viking text and two 'druids' performed the ceremony using ancient stones. 'We even have an official medieval certificate,' says Jane. And even though they are both medieval enthusiasts, and her original wedding dress is now up for sale, she says she hasn't given up hope of a more traditional church wedding at some point in the future. Maybe without the swords.

A CHANCE ENCOUNTER OF A SHOCKING KIND

> **White gold band valued at €4,950. Will sell for €1,000.** Also, 18-carat cluster diamond ring. Brand new, barely worn. Valued at €7,000. I will sell for €1,000. *Evening Echo*

Was €12,000 worth of jewellery for sale for €2,000? It seemed almost too good to be true. 'I need the money because my son needs orthodontic treatment,' the somewhat hesitant voice at the other end of the phone tells me. 'So I thought, time to sell the rings.'

Even though reductions in value are expected in the classifieds, this seemed an extraordinary bargain. I was curious about the price drop, but also the fact that the ad had been placed in the *Evening Echo* and not online. Putting an ad like this online means adding pictures, while a print ad allows greater anonymity and a discreet sale. The words 'brand new' and 'barely worn' coupled with the low price gave me a strong

A Chance Encounter of a Shocking Kind

feeling that there was a story to be told. Initially the seller wasn't sure if she'd feel comfortable meeting me, but a few days after I made contact we did agree to meet.

The interview took place in the car park of a shopping centre and had taken half a dozen phone calls to arrange, including one from a friend of hers checking me out, before it was agreed. I'd given her my car description. When I got there, I scanned the faces exiting the shopping centre to see if I could pick her out from the crowd. Although I'm hopeless at this sort of thing, I find it a useful exercise to try to acknowledge any stereotypes or prejudices I may have before an encounter – even those I'm not conscious of holding.

The seller is a very private person, and it turns out that she has been through a lot in a short space of time. Her experiences have meant that her trust in people she doesn't know, and even in people she does know, has been eroded and is pretty much shattered.

I'm guessing that she's in her early forties and she's of slim build and attractive, with a natural curiosity and an obvious intellect. She sits in the passenger seat of my car, remarking that this is all very strange and she doesn't know quite what she's doing here. On one level it *is* strange to sit in a car with someone you don't know and tell them some of the more intimate details of your life. If I can't meet people in their homes I tend to interview them in my car – sound-wise, it works well and there's a nice informality to it. I sometimes ask interviewees to imagine that we've done the school run and met at the school gate and then they've sat in the car to shelter from the rain for a chat. Then off we go ....

The rings had been given to this woman by her former partner. The relationship ended a long time ago and in her own words, 'Any emotional attachment is long gone.' She says this in a way that's definite, not as if she's trying to convince herself of something, but stating it with certainty and with, to use that awful American phrase, a certain amount of 'closure'.

She tells me that she was in a five-year relationship which produced two children, and as she begins to go into what happened, her hands clench tightly, perhaps mirroring the twist in her stomach, as she revisits what was an incredibly painful time.

She points to the entrance to the large shopping centre. One day, when her daughter was just one, this woman was walking through a clothing store. Another woman passed her and as she did so, she stared at her child. She could see that this passer-by was visibly taken aback. This woman said the child reminded her of her own toddler, who had died a few years previously. In fact, she said, 'She is the spitting image of her.' It was an odd encounter, but both parents chatted away and when the stranger asked her the child's father's name, things took an incredible turn.

A Chance Encounter of a Shocking Kind

'I told her my partner's name,' she says. 'And to my utter shock, she said that was the name of her partner and the father of her child also.' I repeat this slowly so I can process it. 'So out of the blue a woman walked up to you in the shopping centre opposite and said that your child reminded her of her own who had died?' She nods, sharing my incredulity. 'And then it turned out that the children shared a father and you knew nothing about this second family?'

She again nods her head in agreement at the unlikely coincidence. 'I was dumbstruck,' she tells me. 'In that moment, I would possibly have overlooked the fact that he had had a previous relationship that he hadn't told me about. But the fact that he had a child that died, and he didn't tell me about it – that's hugely traumatic.'

The second woman produced a photo of herself, her daughter who had died and the child's father – all three of them together. 'She was like my daughter's twin sister,' she tells me, before adding angrily, 'How could he keep it a secret?' When confronted, his excuse was that he had put his previous family to the back of his mind because of the trauma of losing his child. 'It was something he wanted to forget about as if it didn't happen,' she says.

Some people choose to bury trauma and loss in this way and not share it with those closest to them. But by doing that, they run the risk of the trauma contaminating the good in their lives. While the person opposite me is humane, caring and compassionate, when she realised that her husband had had a previous family she knew nothing about, her first thoughts were not about how deeply his daughter's death must have hurt him if he felt that he had to hide it; she was more concerned that he may have been keeping something else from her. 'So, then I just said, no, let's go our separate ways. This is too bizarre. I was heartbroken at the time, but I'm over it now. I think I dodged a bullet, to be honest.'

She's reluctant to tell me much about her former partner. There is little contact between them now and the fallout from the revelation and the subsequent breakdown of her marriage have made her wary of people. She couldn't contemplate continuing with the relationship once her trust had been broken so fundamentally. The rings, like her former marriage, mean very little to her now. The break-up of her marriage has had other implications, and finding things tough financially, she decided to put the rings up for sale. Any money she receives will be invested in her children's future.

Despite the fact that she has been open about much of the detail, I have a sense that she is holding back large portions of her story. Perhaps this is a coping mechanism to prevent herself from being re-traumatised – and who could blame her?

A Chance Encounter of a Shocking Kind

Her phone flashes, signalling that her children are ready to be collected. I wish her well. Before she gets out of the car she turns to me: 'See, I told you there was a story, didn't I?' she says, before opening the car door and running to embrace her younger child.

A LONG ENGAGEMENT

Stunning wedding dress for sale, size 12–14, never worn. *DoneDeal, September 2016*

'This is the one for sale,' Betty Hornibrook tells me, through the sound of crumpling plastic wrapping, as she removes a large dress from the wardrobe of the spare bedroom in her mid-terrace house.

The front door opens downstairs and she gestures to me to lower my voice while spreading the dress on the bed and flattening it. 'It's a halter neck, right,' she says, in a strong Cork city north side whisper. Carefully, she removes the wrapping to reveal a white dress embellished with beautiful beading. 'You can see the way it falls and the back can be adjusted,' she adds. 'I got it custom made to flatter my figure a bit. When I tried it on – I am 52 years old – I realised I was too old for it. I was like mutton dressed as lamb.'

A Long Engagement

We're whispering because Betty's partner doesn't know she has a dress for sale. He doesn't know she bought it, and he definitely doesn't know that it's a wedding dress, complete with shoes.

And so I make an educated guess that he probably doesn't know about my microphone either, or the fact that I'm upstairs in his home looking at dresses with his life partner. Suddenly I have visions of a six-foot two-inch man, perhaps a former Ford or Dunlop worker, walking up the stairs and seeing his partner and me rummaging through her sock drawer while fumbling for an explanation. In fact, he keeps himself to himself, while I silently try to work out how many bones I'd be likely to break if I had to hurl myself out of the spare bedroom window in a hurry.

Long before we met, Betty had spent hours admiring the dress when it was hanging in her local bridal shop, before finally choosing it, getting it altered and then taking it home and concealing it in the wardrobe. Some time afterwards, when she was on her own in the house, Betty took it out and decided to try it on again. All her wedding dreams, which I later learned had built up over more than three decades, were ruined in that moment when she looked at herself in the mirror. She experienced a flash of clarity when she saw how she looked and made the distinction between reality and fantasy.

'This is a wedding dress to go with an image I had in my head when I was 20 or 30 years old,' she says,

The Personals

reflecting on that moment. 'So I think I am stuck in a time warp and that the mind is not living in the present.' Pointing to her head, she says: 'Up here I'm 30. But the body is 52 and there's no getting away from that. When they are measuring you in the bridal shop, you feel like a million dollars, but then when you get home and you look at yourself properly in the mirror, well, it wasn't me – you know what I mean? It's going to be gorgeous on someone else, but it just wasn't me, like.'

And that really sums up ageing, putting on clothing in your fifties that you would have worn in your twenties, and expecting to look and feel the same but realising that you can't or won't. When Betty looked at herself in the mirror wearing her newly-bought wedding dress, she didn't see herself looking back at her. She saw three decades, two children and three grandchildren in her reflection. Many of us never get that insight, but Betty, who worked hard all her life, left school young and has only ever had one real boyfriend and partner, got all that insight in a split second. The problem was, that insight came at a cost – and a non-refundable one at that.

As with a lot of wedding dresses, because it was custom made, Betty can't return the frock. When we met in late 2016, the wedding was planned for February 2017. The original price of the dress had been €1,600, but it had been reduced to €800 when

A Long Engagement

Betty bought it, and now, weeks after taking it home, she was selling it for €250 or, as she said, 'The best offer I can get.' As I said, insight costs.

Have you had many calls I asked her? 'You're the first call I've got,' she says. I'm not sure I have the hips for it, I joke, and Betty seems somewhat resigned to the fact that she's stuck with this wedding dress she no longer wants.

There is a second part to this story, as there often is with unworn wedding dresses for sale. Betty did buy another dress, and it's one that she feels more comfortable in. She dives into another wardrobe to retrieve it, like a heron on the Lee seizing its lunch, and she takes it out and shows it to me. Now, I'm no Vera Wang, but to my eye it did look more streamlined – classier, I would say – and although I'm really stretching my wedding attire knowledge to the limit here, not so typically bridal.

In terms of the backstory, you might be forgiven for thinking that at 52 perhaps Betty is on her second marriage, or maybe she just never found the right partner, or perhaps she is a widow. But her reason for getting married in her fifties is more complex. We're still whispering as Betty continues to speak passionately about the dress on her bed. So much so, wide hips or no wide hips, I'm really coming round to the idea of buying it myself, I tell her. We both laugh and then she hushes me. We have to call a halt to the

The Personals

whispering, I tell her. I mean, what's the big deal – surely her partner knows all by now?

'No, he doesn't even know I have two dresses, right? *He. Doesn't. Even. Know. I. Have. Two. Dresses*,' she says, emphasising each word the second time round.

'You're 52,' I say, 'and he's what age?'

'He's 58.'

'You've been engaged how long?'

'For 35 years.'

Three and a half decades of an engagement. Fair enough, we all like to test out a product before buying it, but this is taking it a bit far, surely? Betty laughs. All round the house are photos of her family which she shows me with pride. She's open and friendly, and happy to go into the story of what must be one of the longest engagements in Ireland.

The story starts in 1982 when Betty and her partner first got engaged. She was 17 and her fiancé asked her father if they could get married. 'My father chased him and said get out of it. You're too old. She's too young,' Betty explains. 'You see, my sister had got married the year before and so my father was after a big wedding, and he wasn't going throwing more money at another one so that I would end up back home again, as he saw it. But I didn't come home, did I? We just moved out then and got our own place and the story began from there.'

A Long Engagement

The 1980s were such a different time, when fathers still had that kind of control over their daughters and could refuse to bless a marriage. And now 35 years on Betty has two children with her fiancé. William is 32 and Scott is 22. She wants me to mention her lovely daughter-in-law, Audrey, and the fact that she also has three beautiful grandchildren.

From the age of 17 onwards, Betty had always had it in mind to get married, but life events got in the way. 'The plan was we'll do it this time, or we'll do it that time, but something always came up. So, I think now it's our time. Food is booked, music is booked and we're going to have a lovely day.' I can't help wondering though, for a couple who have been together so long – for decades, in fact – what difference will it make getting married?

'I'll tell you now, he's my best friend,' she says, 'and I'm quite sure I would be his best friend. He understands me and I understand him and we just adore the children and the grandchildren. It has been a lifelong dream of ours and we just want to fulfil it.' If Betty doesn't shift the dress, she says she will donate it to a charity. I meet her fiancé briefly as I'm leaving the house, and it's endearing that he's not afraid to show his affection for Betty in front of a stranger. She says she'll tell him all later, as I scuttle towards the exit. Some weeks later I drop in and we laugh and chat about it.

The Personals

A few months after that, Betty messaged me to say that on 10 February 2017, she and her partner walked to the GAA club opposite their home and had their wedding. All their family were there, including the grandkids, and the bride wore a simple yet classy evening dress. The kind of dress that is timeless. 'It was,' Betty says, 'one of the greatest days of my life.'

Her first wedding dress, by the way, is still for sale.

ADDICTED TO LOVE?

Hand-wrought platinum wedding and engagement rings for sale. Brilliant cut diamonds in a channel setting. Matching set. €7,500. *DoneDeal, August 2018*

As a single mother with a busy work life, Paula had originally planned that her brother would sell her two platinum diamond rings and that she would give him a commission in return.

She liked the distance this gave her from the transaction, and couldn't face the thought of walking into one of those 'cash for gold' outlets and handing over her jewellery to be examined and valued. She lives in a small community, and felt doing that would make something deeply personal and traumatic become too public.

Thinking back, one of the signs of deepening recession in 2008 was that 'cash for gold' counters began appearing in shopping centres with little by way of screens to protect the privacy of customers. I remember seeing four women queueing up in Merchants Quay in Cork to get their rings valued in late 2009, as the recession was taking hold. Having ruled out that option, Paula's brother persuaded her to put the rings on DoneDeal.

Initially in the months after her marriage ended, Paula spoke to the shop where the rings were bought, and floated the idea of the shop buying them back. Both rings had been custom made but she had thought she could get them turned into something else, or that the jewellers could recycle them into a ring for another person. These were Celtic Tiger-era rings bought for a significant sum so the materials carried value.

'I had a fair idea of what they cost,' she tells me. 'I didn't know the exact figure, but it was substantial. They meant much more to me than monetary value. I am not really into jewellery but I suppose they were particularly significant in what they symbolised. Now though, they are the opposite of that. They are just metal and stone and I wouldn't want to even pass them on to my daughter. I just think now they were given to me under false pretences. People always say, "Love is blind", but now I know what that means.'

Paula is in her early forties and had been in a relationship with her ex-husband for much of her adult life. When we spoke, the break-up was still quite raw.

Addicted to Love?

Her voice fragmented with emotion several times during our conversation. The primary aim for her in selling the rings wasn't really financial gain, but more an emotional one. 'My husband had an addiction. He had more than one actually,' Paula tells me. 'I discovered there was a lot of unfaithfulness before and during the marriage. I realised this early on into the marriage when I found another phone. He didn't admit to it 100 per cent, but there was enough evidence to go for counselling. He still didn't admit to it or anything, he just said it was a bit of texting and fun,' she explains.

Initially, Paula says her husband was very apologetic and reassured her that the phone messages meant nothing. He was proactive in terms of addressing the issues he had and he seemed genuine about doing whatever it took to keep the relationship going. 'I thought, OK, we'll go for counselling and it will be fine. Looking back, I was so stupid,' she says.

Paula thinks her husband loved her for periods of the time they were together, but that commitment and monogamy weren't a priority for him. 'Maybe he didn't want to continue the infidelity. I think actually, looking back, he probably had a sex addiction. That was just one more addiction to add to his list of them.'

Despite the issues she'd identified their relationship continued and Paula soon became pregnant with the couple's first child. 'He was so manipulative,' she says. 'I was busy and didn't notice as much and I was easy-going, so I suppose I let things slide, but his drinking got worse, day by day. His addictions were much worse than the infidelity to deal with. Addiction is the hardest thing I've ever dealt with.'

This was something I could relate to personally. Fifteen years ago, I had gone into rehab, mainly for alcohol issues, and I subsequently wrote a book detailing both my relationship with alcohol – and Ireland's too. My life had gone off-piste when I walked into a rehab centre in west Cork called Tabor Lodge. Through intensive counselling and with the help of some fellow addicts who shared some of their journey with me, I began to piece things back together bit by bit. I have been lucky. The closest I have come to a slip was a Baileys' cheesecake at a wedding a few years ago, and in the decade and a half since rehab I've always been drawn to addicts and their stories. It's tough being an addict anywhere, but it's perhaps doubly tough in Ireland, a country which arguably stigmatises sobriety far more than active addiction. The bar is set incredibly high for someone to identify as an addict in Ireland. In fact, if anything, all the societal impulses are telling you that you're not really that bad. As the writer Conor McPherson once told me, walk into a bar in Ireland and the guy at the counter drinking Ballygowan, that's the alcoholic!

Addicted to Love?

Since I went public about my fraught relationship with alcohol, many individuals and families have contacted me over the years, asking for advice or help with their own struggles. Many are fearful of the societal response to publicly acknowledging their issue and seeking help. This particularly applies to Irish men over a certain age, for whom a large part of their formative experiences may have been framed using alcohol as a buttress. The difficulty for loved ones around addicts is just how deceptive, manipulative and destructive the addicted person can be.

'According to him, I was the only problem he had in his life,' Paula says, reflecting on her ex-husband's outlook. 'He would probably sit you down and if you didn't know he was my ex, you would believe everything he says. He is almost a split person. He can be an amazing, charming and really kind person, and then he is awful. So it's the total ends of the scale, and unfortunately, there was more of the awful behaviour than the nice person as time went on.'

Paula says she tried everything to get her husband to face up to his addiction, even managing to persuade him to go to a rehab facility for an assessment. This did not end well as he wouldn't accept the opinion of the professionals. 'I remember his face,' she says. 'He was in complete disbelief and then afterwards, he said it was what I said before the assessment that made them decide he was an alcoholic. He was that much in denial about it. He would deny all the affairs, even when a woman came to me and confessed she was with him and she broke up with him because of the guilt. She confessed to everything and he was still denying it to me.'

Denial, not just a river in Egypt, as we used to say in rehab. But for Paula, it's almost easier to accept her husband's behaviour, knowing that he does have an addiction. 'I think I would be very angry with him if he was behaving like this and he wasn't an addict,' she says. 'I am more forgiving and understanding now, though, and it is easier to accept that he is not a completely black soul. I just think now that maybe it is the addiction that has made him the way he is.'

His drinking was becoming a daily problem and then, in addition to the emotional abuse, he was physically violent. Eventually she plucked up the courage to go to her solicitor and seek a separation. Any emotional ties she had had with him had long since been cut by this point, and physically, she and her ex-husband had been apart for some time. His actions from the day she told him she wanted a separation convinced her that she had done the right thing.

'I didn't have to open my mouth; the truth all came out and not from me. I am a very private person,' she says. 'While all this was happening, a woman told me about the affair she had been having with my husband for two and a half years. She then wrote me a letter and said if I ever needed it for anything legal to use it. What she did was so courageous. I know her quite well. I thought we were kind of friends. She didn't really get on with other mothers and the irony is I used to make an extra effort with her. Little did I know ...'

To anyone looking in from the outside, Paula's husband seemed a highly functioning individual. He was careful only to drink at night but it became apparent after several years that he had lost a lot of work opportunities. He could have done so well, she says, but his dependence on alcohol held him back hugely. Despite all his faults, her son still very much looks up to her ex-husband. She hasn't tried to influence his opinion of his father; she says he will figure that out for himself some day.

After all she has gone through, including emerging from an abusive relationship, I'm curious as to why Paula has decided that this is the right time to put her rings online and try to sell them. The break-up is still relatively recent. 'If I don't, I'm afraid I will lose them, or they could get stolen,' she says. 'He could also take them back, and I thought if I do sell them, it will provide a fund for the kids' education. It would be something positive, and I'm a big believer in turning negatives into positives.'

The whole experience and ongoing fallout from the break-up of her relationship has impacted on Paula's ability to make future connections and relationships.

The Personals

'I don't think I ever want to get into a relationship again,' she tells me. 'I think he would have to be extraordinary for me to even look at him twice! I feel like I wasted many years, but I learned so much and I am proud of myself for coming out of it. I question everything now when people talk to me. My eyes have been opened and I can't believe how gullible I was. My faith helped me. When I was outside the door, crying into my hands after a bout of abuse, I would cry out, "Please God, help me" and He did, and along the way, I found groups like Al Anon really useful, to be honest.'

At her worst, Paula was afraid her husband's drinking would drag her down with him, and depression would become an issue for her. She says she came from a very happy family: both parents were non-drinkers and theirs was an open house in the country. It was the kind of childhood home where they drank tea five or six times a day and everyone was open and honest with each other. 'I often wonder how I did not see that these traits were missing in the person I married. How did I miss that? If by me going through this though, I prevent my kids falling into addiction, then maybe it will have been worth it.'

We've been talking for almost an hour, and Paula tells me she has to do the school run and needs to go. I thank her for her time, openness and honesty.

I came away from our phone call thinking that it was relatively soon after her break-up for her to be

Addicted to Love?

selling the rings online and that in my experience most people travel a few years down the road before they take that step.

A few days after our chat, when I noticed the ad had expired, I texted, asking whether she'd had any luck with a buyer. 'I decided to take the ad down,' she tells me. 'I just thought, maybe I should think about this more. I didn't want total strangers contacting me and then having to explain the backstory. I'm just not ready to face all that right now.'

A MARRIAGE WORTH WAITING FOR

> **For sale: beautiful NEW ivory wedding dress.** NEVER WORN or altered. Size 18. Seeing this dress is a must. Will sell half price: was €1,400, sell for €800. No time-wasters. *Evening Echo, October 2018*

It had been a while since I'd come across a wedding dress ad in the free ads section of the *Evening Echo*. There had been a time when bridal wear had a whole section to itself. However, online ads allow sellers to post pictures of items for sale and many online classified sections allow more control, as you don't have to use your real name or publish your phone number if you choose not to. And this can be very important when someone is selling a dress for a wedding that never happened. So the fact this ad was in the *Echo* at all caught my eye straight away, and then when the words 'NEW' and 'NEVER WORN'

A Marriage Worth Waiting For

also appeared in the advert, I knew there was likely to be a story.

The seller, Jean, tells me that this is the second time she's put this ad in the newspaper. The dress cost her €1,400 and she's letting it go for €800, or the nearest offer. 'Myself and my husband planned to get married,' she tells me. 'But I was already married and I thought the divorce would be through by then. But the divorce didn't come through until [years after]. It actually went on for about 14 years whereas normally divorces should only take five years.'

The divorce finally came through seven years after Jean and her partner had hoped to get married. By this stage, organising a wedding that would keep everyone in each family happy was proving difficult to say the least. Also, both Jean and her husband had lost their jobs as the recession hit, and so their big dream wedding had to be shelved out of economic necessity.

These are the ripple effects of the downturn that still resonated many years after the so-called recovery had taken hold. It is almost impossible to calculate the whole impact of the recession – you can document the numbers: who left, the people out of work or the families who had their homes repossessed, but for years after the downturn, I met people like Jean who would tell me about the ways in which the economic tsunami (not of their making) had massively changed the course of their lives.

The Personals

People have told me about the son or daughter in Australia they couldn't visit for half a decade. Or the retirement plan that never materialised, or the family member languishing on a waiting list for five years for a hip replacement, because one of the first things to go after the crash had been their health insurance. How do you properly assess the cumulative impact of all those knock-on effects?

For some, the recession had a more positive impact ultimately, forcing them perhaps to go off and spend a month at the Ballymaloe Cookery School and do what they should have done 30 years earlier before the entry exams for the bank came up. In some cases, it helped people embrace humility, or discover empathy or form a kinship with people from a whole cross section of backgrounds which they might never have thought possible. I met them at Men's Sheds, car boot sales, coming out of the repossession courts or, unfortunately, at coroners' courts. They were all marked in some way by the events following the collapse of a bank many had probably never even heard of.

So after the collapse of Lehman Brothers bank in 2008, when Jean and her fiancé were talking about their dream wedding, perhaps with the three-day venue and the chocolate fountain and the dozen doves being released, their plans didn't seem in keeping with the times. Both of them were out of work. Her husband had retrained and ended up starting at the bottom of his profession on minimum wage, trying to work his way up again. Jean says that they had both been on an upward curve financially before the recession. Once they lost their jobs, things began to slide very quickly. Soon they were in mortgage arrears and they continue to struggle to clear those arrears to this day. They face the prospect of losing their home.

'I don't know what's going to happen,' Jean tells me. 'We've been paying half what we should be paying. We can't do any more than that. It has had a huge impact on our lives. We don't go out socially and in terms of holidays, we go camping for a week every year. I have a tent I bring with us and that's our holiday. Financially, we are so much worse off since the recession, but thankfully my kids have grown up so it's just us and the dog to look after.'

With money tight, and having lived together for quite a while, the big spectacular wedding was not going to work out. So what did they do? 'We flew to [the Caribbean] and got married there,' Jean tells me. 'We took one suitcase and the whole thing cost us €3,800 for two weeks. I left the wedding dress I bought behind and ended up buying another dress for €400 – one that I could wear on the beach because I had outgrown the first one. It was absolutely magical.'

Feck off recession, in other words.

By the time Jean got married for the second time, she was well over 40. Her first marriage had lasted

The Personals

over a decade, and while she and her current husband have been married for several years, they have been together a lot longer. There's a reason they had to wait so long to get married which I'll come to, but looking back, Jean is now able to see clearly why her first marriage failed. 'I was very young when I got married first time,' she tells me. 'Too young, to be honest. I was 19 years of age going on 20. I only knew him about eight months. My own mother got married at 17, so it was the done thing back then. I was in love and he was my first serious boyfriend.'

Jean's father had died when she was 17. He had still been a young man. Looking back on it she says she endured a very controlled upbringing in which her father had a strong hand in her personal life, something that's probably totally alien to today's teenagers. This meant she had to be in bed most nights at 9 p.m. and had very little choice to do anything socially. So when her father died, she naturally responded to her newfound freedom.

'I went a bit crazy and I was a bit of a handful for my mother,' she says. 'The environment was so strict for me when I was younger. All my friends would be going out dancing in the local hall over the weekend. I'd come into school Monday and I wasn't even allowed to go to the cinema or the shops hardly. I had nothing to talk to them about. Parents think by doing this they are keeping their kids closer to them and shaping better what they want them to be, but in reality, they are pushing them away and into the thing they fear most.'

Although Jean married young, at first it went well, but after a few years problems arose. She and her ex-husband split up at one stage and she says she went back to him because he promised he'd change. She spent several more years living with him, time she now says was a 'waste'. 'I went back believing things would change and they didn't,' she adds.

She met her present husband out socially. Every Thursday night she used to go with a friend to a local bar. Her husband was from a large family and she knew his sister-in-law and they would pass each other from time to time in the bar. One night he joined them. She was still living with her previous husband at the time. 'I was with him physically, but emotionally, I wasn't with him. We hadn't shared a room in a long time.' Jean and I discuss how often people think they're doing the right thing by children in staying together, but how often this can have a far greater negative impact than adults realise. Reflecting back, she said her children became pawns at times in the disagreements between her and her ex-husband, especially after their separation.

Having left her husband, she had her wedding to her new partner to plan. A deposit was paid and the limousine was booked. Jean had assumed that divorces took up to five years to complete, when you take into account the time they had spent living apart, and then the time needed to go through the legal process. Instead, the process dragged on for several years more, as difficulties between her and her ex-husband played themselves out in court. This meant that much like her teenage years, her life was on hold again. Eventually the process was complete and she attended court for one final time to have her divorce finalised.

'I will never forget that day,' she says. 'I went to the courtroom and the judge said to me, what do you want? He meant financially, but I told him all I wanted was my divorce, nothing else. The judge said I was entitled to certain things, but I just said please give me my freedom. I walked out of that courtroom feeling as happy as if I had won the lottery.'

Within a few weeks, the wedding was back on, but now they could only afford a much smaller gathering of about 30 or so guests. This did not go down well with either extended family. At this point she and her partner had been living together for well over a decade, and the hassle about numbers and who would be left out was turning her off the idea of marriage. 'It was really important to my husband that we get married,' she tells me. 'As far as I was concerned we were a married couple anyway, but he thought differently. If I suggested not getting married, he would say, "Don't you love me enough to marry me?" He's a lot younger than me.'

A Marriage Worth Waiting For

Her husband got his wish and they committed to each other on a beach in the Caribbean where she wore a light summer dress. The dress for sale in the ad is a heavy chiffon dress more suited to Irish weather, and comes with a large train. When she took it out to photograph it, part of her still regretted not getting married in it. If she sells the dress, the money will be spent on children, grandchildren and great-grandchildren. She may not have had the wedding she wanted, but she says in the end she ended up in the marriage she wanted. 'I come first as far as my husband is concerned,' she tells me, proudly. 'He puts up with me and he is very quiet in fairness. I could nag the life out of him and he never reacts. The most he might say is "bite me" or something off-hand like that.'

The secret to a happy relationship she says is to marry someone who is a friend first and with whom you share similar interests. She says that looking back, she and her first husband were too similar in terms of their strong personalities. 'You almost have to have one person in the relationship who compromises a lot,' she says.

She says she can't think of a single complaint she would make about her husband – he is the love of her life and her best friend. 'He is so easy-going,' she tells me. 'He never says anything bad or is ever coming out against me. If I said to him jump off a bridge, he would do it if he thought it would please me. And that's

The Personals

saying something, because the same fella has an awful fear of water ...'

Part Two

EQUIPPED FOR LIFE

THE CAR THAT'S BULLETPROOF

For sale: armoured car – can withstand a 9mm, .38 Special, .44 Magnum and all smaller calibre ammunition as well as a small bomb. *Irish Independent, 2015*

It's not every day you see an armoured car for sale. And this was in the *Irish Independent* classified section, where I've rarely found stories. So, one Friday in 2015, I went to the west of Ireland to meet the seller, an Eastern European who told me he had imported the car. It had cost €100,000 when manufactured, and he was hoping to get €15,000. A bargain, surely. So how could I tell it is armoured?

'OK, if you go around the car with me and lift the door, for example, you see how heavy it is,' he explains in a pronounced west of Ireland accent. 'You can also knock on the roof of the car. It's not empty, it's like knocking on concrete. Rock solid.'

The Personals

And it really was rock solid – the thing must have weighed several tonnes and here it was in a car park outside an industrial estate, having been imported some months earlier. Who had owned it previously, I asked. 'It belonged to an Italian government minister,' he told me.

Assuming that it's a little on the heavy side for the school run, who in the name of God wants an armoured car in Ireland? 'People who can afford it,' he says, ever the salesman. He's done this before, clearly. Sensing my scepticism, he goes on. 'You see Irish people have the wrong perception of armoured cars and only associate them with criminals. I would say 80 per cent of people who buy armoured cars are from the government or NGOs.'

And while he's telling me this, I have a vision of an Irish cleric turned NGO worker driving around in this bombproof, armour-plated BMW, the latest Snoop Dogg album on high volume, cruising through the ghetto that is Mount Melleray or Glenstal Abbey.

There's a serious point here: given the recent spate of gangland killings in Dublin, how can the seller verify that the person buying it from him is doing so for purely legal reasons or activities?

'This is not a piece of military equipment,' he says defiantly. 'We will do a Garda check on somebody. Everything is bulletproof. Windows, doors and the roof. It's the first armoured car I've brought into

The Car That's Bulletproof

Ireland, but I've sold lots of other armoured cars over the years so I know what I'm doing. Lots of them sold to the Middle East and a few of them sold to America and Canada.'

I sit in the driver's seat and turn the key, get her ticking over just to hear the sound of the engine and feel the weight under me. It starts on cue and sounds good for a car weighing 2.7 tonnes and laden with armour plating and bombproof windows.

A few weeks later, I phone to find out how he'd got on. Did a curate or a criminal try to buy it? 'I got no calls,' he tells me. 'So I had to export it back to Eastern Europe. It seems there's not much demand among Irish government ministers for armoured cars.'

'You were about 100 years too late, mate,' I tell him.

FOR YOUR EYES ONLY

For sale: eavesdropping bug for hidden voice recording, transmits up to about 200 square metres and can enable listening through a wall. *Evening Echo*

The seller behind what must be one of the strangest ads I've seen would only meet me at a petrol station, and gave me instructions to park in a part which was flooded with light. She was very specific in her directions and I suspect she parked some distance away and observed me for a few minutes before walking over to my car.

She was very polite, and happy to tell me something of the backstory to the items and the ad. She didn't grow up in Ireland, she told me, sitting in the passenger seat, but she had moved here some years previously. Once we were convinced that neither of us was a double agent, we travelled to a remote country cottage where she was living. She offered me poached eggs, which was weird. It was 6 p.m. I declined and instead she made a cup of tea, and then sat down in her living room, where she began to unpack several items from large cardboard boxes piled up against one wall.

I could scarcely believe what I was seeing as she laid out a spy camera pen, a false smoke detector with a hidden camera, a pair of reading glasses also with a camera hidden in them, and a listening device that could pick up conversations from 45 metres away. By the time all the items were unpacked, thousands of euros worth of high-tech surveillance equipment was laid out in front of me, all of which had been put up for sale in the classified ads from time to time.

'I bought all this for a particular reason,' she tells me, 'and I had a hard time finding these in the first place. While it was difficult to locate this equipment, I am having a harder time selling them.'

The seller came to Ireland a few years ago for a holiday. She had worked in a fast-paced work environment in the private sector and needed to get away for a while and had thought Ireland would be calm and peaceful. While on a two-week break, she fell in love with the place – mainly the countryside – and thought that the slower pace of life would be a nice change, so she decided to stay for a few months after that. 'Somehow along the way I met somebody – a local man,' she tells me. 'I rented a house from him,

The Personals

actually. We began a relationship and later, we decided to get married. But before that, while I was renting from him, I found out his own marriage was not a regular marriage, in the sense that the wife was not there. They had separated. He was trying to get access to some money in an account that he told me belonged to both of them and he told me he was left with a mortgage to pay.'

Because of the divorce laws here, she says they had to contact the man's ex-wife as they needed to show that she had lived away from the family home for a period of time. At some point his ex-wife returned, and disputes began between the parties and it became difficult to verify the truth of what either was saying. After these disagreements, there were conflicting accounts of what was said and the tone of the engagements.

'Every time after she came to the house she would make accusations,' she said. 'I wanted proof that this is not true, you see, so I searched around for stuff to film covertly. Our idea was to make some recordings and some covert filming so that if she said at one point in time or date that he was doing something to her or they were arguing in a certain way, then we wanted to prove at that point in time he was somewhere else or it didn't happen that way.'

And so she trawled the internet for something that would help prove that her partner was behaving correctly. The idea for surveillance equipment came via Hollywood. 'We were on the couch watching Irish TV, and one of the Bond movies was on, one of the old ones,' she tells me. 'In my head, I was thinking about all the stuff we were dealing with and I thought, wait a minute, I can buy these things to take footage just like James Bond so I hunted around to buy it and take the footage.'

It's somewhat surreal to be sitting in this cottage in rural Ireland hearing that James Bond inspired this woman to become a sleuth. I tell her I admire her resourcefulness.

Eventually she says an order was made that the house should be split between both parties, and that her partner should leave the house while their assets were divided. The situation continued for a few years until they were able to buy back the house and move in again. All seemed to be fine, and finally life for the new couple could begin. She thought about getting rid of the equipment then, but held on to it and the footage she had gathered just in case it was ever needed.

And, sure enough, one day some months later, someone from social welfare called at their door, looking to confirm some details, as they were concerned the address was being used to make claims, including for disability. 'The welfare inspector asked me for any tapes or CCTV we had associated with the house. He wanted it to prove that the person claiming wasn't

The Personals

entitled to do so. Eventually there was a charge and a prosecution and we've had very little contact since,' she says.

And so, not needing the surveillance equipment any longer, she has been trying to sell it for some months through the classified section of the *Evening Echo*. Had she had many phone calls? 'I had one call and I sold one item. It was sad, actually,' she tells me. 'The man who bought it said that he suspected his wife was having an affair and he wanted proof so he could confront her about it. He called here and I took out some of the equipment and showed him how you work it. In the end, he bought the button camera. I don't know how he got on afterwards. To be honest, I don't really want to know.'

That had been over a year before our chat and since then she hasn't had one phone call. When I ask if she is worried that someone may buy this equipment for the wrong reasons, she assures me she is careful to screen prospective buyers. I'm not sure how well you can screen people in practice, but I guess if someone really wants this equipment they can buy it online anonymously anyway. She begins to pack up the items, carefully putting each piece of surveillance equipment back in its box. I'm left wondering why anyone would want to buy this stuff, aside from trying to find out if their partner was having an affair – and how much it would cost them.

For Your Eyes Only

'People may need it for security, or to gather evidence in case you ever need it, like we did,' she says. 'I'm selling parts of it for €160 but it's worth more than that and I don't mean in terms of monetary value. Frankly, you can't put a price on your integrity and honour. You know with this kind of thing you only look for it when you really need it. You might think it's James Bond type stuff, but it exists and it can really change your life.'

RUNNING UP THAT HILL

Power chair for sale. Adult size 20. Complete with charger, manual and receipt. Bought for €10,200. In excellent condition. Genuine reasons for selling. €6,500 ono. *Evening Echo, October 2018*

Last April, I was in my sitting room when I got a phone call to say that one of my closest friends – the musician and songwriter Brian Carey – had died. I'd thought there was some mistake, that the caller, a mutual friend, had mixed me up with someone else. He'd got the number wrong maybe or this was some elaborate hoax or prank. Good one. Ha. Ha. Ha.

I remember having to sit down on the couch to physically take the details on board. Brian was dead. The friend was sorry. It looked like, well, you know ... There wasn't much more he could say. The coded unsaid was clear.

Running Up That Hill

Brian and I had been friends for about 17 years. We were both blow-ins to Cork. He was from Dublin, I from Ennis and we shared something of an outsider's view of our adopted city. We both became fathers at roughly the same time. We lived together at times, took a holiday together, shared a passion for boxing and Bob Dylan. Over the years, we'd developed our own wink and nod language of delight, our own shorthand, and had jokes that ran for years, pretending often that we were old prize fighters ready at any moment to come out of retirement. 'I think you've still got a little bit left in the basement, Brian,' he would say, as I'd shadow box fervently and we'd both break into laughter.

Brian came to my fortieth birthday party that summer, and as he always did, brought his guitar and played and sang. On birthdays, weddings, New Year's Eve, Brian was always there with a guitar. I knew his songs by heart and many of them are now on a YouTube channel he created. Of course, when I listen to them now all I can hear is depression. Like this one, for example, called 'Running Up That Hill'.

> And you know sometimes we can admit
> That all the barriers broken down
> Just how hard it can get
> When the walls we build are too high to climb
> And you know sometimes you can escape

The Personals

> When all the days they're so ordinary
> The wind blows hard but who can tell
> When there's every which way to turn
> Oh, yeah, I know
> We're only running up that hill
> Only to find
> There's nothing there ...

Ultimately the hill proved too high for my friend. In the days and weeks after Brian died the grief hit me in waves, crashing violently at first, unrelenting, then getting into its own rhythm, ebbing and flowing. I could have done more. I should have done more. Why hadn't I been more present? The day he died I had been working very close to his house and it had crossed my mind to call on him. I didn't. We hadn't seen each other much in the weeks before he died. Now I know it was because he was struggling. I wasn't alert enough to it. Suicide leaves so many questions, and part of me will always feel guilt. I'll always feel I could have done more, could have been a better friend, could have saved him. Looking back, there are things I would have done differently.

Grief is a strange emotion. After the initial days and weeks passed, I remember sitting one day in a coffee shop in Cork and thinking that grief was actually quite a beautiful thing on one level. It takes you by the hand and shows you how much you really cared for someone. It led me to a new awareness about what grief is, how it can dominate your life if you let it and how you have to learn to live with your grief, to own it and to form your own personal relationship with it. 'Grief,' said Queen Elizabeth II, 'is the price we pay for love' and that's probably the one standout quote that has stuck with me since.

So now when I see ads like the one at the start of this piece, I'm more attuned to the possibility that grief may be stalking the lives of the sellers, hanging around each line of the ad like a heavy fog that is slow to lift. I phone the number.

'I'm in Aldi, can we talk a little later on?' says the voice on the other end of the line. The accent is a mix of Cork and Kerry, the kind of accent you'll hear on YouTube clips of old IRA volunteers talking about ambushes in Ballyvourney or Kanturk. There were a few signposts in the ad that drew me in. First, the fact that the chair is in 'excellent' condition suggests it wasn't used all that long, hinting perhaps at a recent bereavement or maybe, with luck, a miraculous recovery.

'Genuine reasons for selling' usually means that the seller is not a dealer or someone who buys items cheaply in order to sell them on for a profit. It's more usually someone who had to buy something without much preparation, and now wishes to dispense with it. Often it's someone who has experienced a significant event and now, after a little time and distance, feels ready to take a step forward.

An hour or two after our initial phone call, when the Aldi run is complete and the car is presumably loaded with bags of German jam, power drills and wetsuits, we speak by phone again.

Julia has a voice which is warm and open, and she seems to have time to talk which, in this era of instant messaging when people don't even have the time to leave voice messages, is really refreshing. She tells me the chair had sold a week earlier and made €5,000, just under half the original purchase price. She had been reluctant to place the ad, and before doing so had phoned a number of health and charitable organisations wondering if they would buy the relatively new motorised chair from her.

To Julia's surprise, there was no way to recycle the chair, even though she makes the point that regular wheelchairs and walkers were recycled by the health services all the time. So, in part spurred on by desperation and exasperation, she turned to the small ads. We talked a little about that, and also about the different view of the world you get when a loved one starts using a wheelchair. She was struck by how footpaths and roads present obstacles, and how people, both consciously and subconsciously, look at you differently.

The wheelchair belonged to her husband, Julia tells me, and shortly after he began using it they went away for a weekend to a hotel, which he had booked. 'When we went to check in, the person at the desk would automatically speak to me, even though the hotel booking was in my husband's name,' she tells me. 'In our local area, after my husband began using the wheelchair, some people would look at us and not even say hello and just keep going. It was so strange.'

Julia tells me that her husband had had health problems most of his adult life, and added to this, he had suffered a number of strokes and then a heart attack. His health difficulties eventually resulted in him having both his legs amputated, which had a devastating physical and psychological effect on him. He had been an incredibly active sports person, the kind of man who would be comfortable parachuting out of a helicopter. To go from that high level of activity to sitting in a chair all day long meant a huge adjustment for him and for her, she tells me.

While all this was happening, Julia was dealing with a lot of grief in her other relationships. In the space of 12 months she lost her mother and two close friends, and then her brother came through a battle with throat cancer. You have to stay positive, she says, and initially at least the wheelchair was a real plus in their lives. 'It was fantastic in that he was able to go around the shop on his own,' she says. 'It did bring its own problems though, and again things you don't think about beforehand, like how high items are on shelves and how hard it is for someone in a wheelchair to reach them. But you learn to live and adapt.'

The first bolt of grief to hit Julia had come in January 2015 when her father passed away suddenly. It had been a massive shock to the family, and the first time she and her seven siblings had had to deal with grief. Following that, in April 2015, her husband had had his foot amputated, and then just over a year later, in June 2016, his second one was also removed. Shortly after that, her mother had passed away. No sooner had one wave of grief hit when she had to brace herself for another and another. 'It was a really difficult few years,' she says. 'If I actually sat down and thought about it chronologically, I would probably crack up. I don't know how I'm still here,' she adds candidly.

Just as she was getting over that series of traumas, in June 2017 Julia's husband passed away. She tells me that you have to look at the positive side of grief. She thinks back to the morning her husband died, for example. 'There were two rapid response personnel and two ambulances at the house the day he died. It was unbelievable the support I got,' she says. 'They worked on him and had all these machines in the house and they kept me updated on what was going on. They held my hand and really helped me through it. When it happened, I felt happy for him. Every day, he was in constant pain and each morning a new pain was added to his existing ones. The last few months were really hard.'

At this point we break off and begin to chat about the merits or otherwise of euthanasia. I tell Julia about an old college friend who travelled to Switzerland when the pain of his condition became too much and ended his life in a clinic there. I saw something of the suffering he underwent and could perfectly understand his decision. But I tell her, having experienced the sheer emotional devastation of suicide, I've also seen the incredibly destructive impact that ending one's own life can have on those who are left behind as they struggle to piece the meaning of that sharp ending together. I tell her I feel conflicted about the issue.

Julia feels no such conflict when she reflects on the way her husband suffered towards the end. 'I totally agree with euthanasia,' she tells me. 'I would vote for it without a doubt. For people who suffer towards the end it is so horrific for them. With my own mother and father, they both got sick just three months before the end and that was it. It was short. My father was 78 and my mother was 80 and they were largely healthy and happy people and lived lovely lives. But there is in a way a form of euthanasia in Ireland; we just don't speak about it.'

When talking about grief, sometimes people fall into a pattern of asking if calendar events such as

The Personals

Christmas will be tougher than usual. A lot of focus is placed on anniversaries and particular times of the year when the family would have been together. For what it's worth, if grief has taught me anything, it's that sometimes it's not the big life events that are the most difficult to cope with. It's the rainy Tuesday in February when a musty smell brings the person back into your life, or the way someone clears leaves from a driveway on an autumn day, or a seaside sound or a song fragment in a shopping centre lift. And while birthdays, Christmases, weddings and all those life events can be difficult, very often grief is hiding in the mundane.

When you've cared for someone who was sick for a long time, adjusting to life without them can be difficult, but the adjustment to a life in which you no longer care for them can be equally difficult. 'I had an hour a day to myself for the past five years,' Julia tells me. 'That was when the home help came in and I would take that hour and go to the shops. I now have a new lease of life. I don't mean it to sound like I was a prisoner in my own home but I've gone from basically providing 24/7 care to nothing. It's a really big change.'

She says she's one of the lucky ones in that she did get to say goodbye properly before her husband died. About a week before he passed, he was lying in bed and she was sitting in a chair next to him. He motioned to her to lean in closer to her and then he whispered through strained breaths: 'I really do love you.' Julia choked up and didn't really know what to say. He'd caught her off guard in between fretting about making him comfortable and ensuring his needs were met as humanely as possible. 'I just said jokingly, "Sure I love me too." He then said something else and I don't know what it was, but I said to him, "Do you think you're dying?" He said, "Yes" for the first time, and I again just passed it off with a joke, something along the lines of, "You'll bury me yet."'

Looking back now she says that over the next few days there were tell-tale signs that he was losing his fight against illness. At two o'clock in the morning on one of those days she went in to check on him and she says he was having a loud chat with himself and laughing. When she asked who he was talking to, he said his parents, both of whom had died decades earlier. Julia says she hopes she's not being too graphic but she wants to tell me what the end was like.

Living in a rural area, with the post office and the pub and the local corner shop under threat, the opportunity for conversation becomes limited. So while it might seem strange that someone I have never met is relaying the most intimate details of her and her late husband's final moments together, it felt to me that she had stored all this up, waiting for the moment someone asked her – really asked her – how it was. Sometimes too it's easier to tell a stranger.

The Personals

'When I went in and he was talking to his parents, I discovered he had soiled himself and the bed needed to be changed,' she tells me. 'I do know now this is what they sometimes call the final run, if you know what I mean. At the time, I was thinking how will I clean this up now without upsetting him? That's the kind of thing that goes through your mind. So, I said to him, "I'm going to get a basin and tidy up a bit, and then after that, I will make a nice cup of tea for us." While he wasn't looking, I slipped off the sheets and pillows and changed them. I was glad the way I dealt with it; he had his dignity intact. Twenty-four hours later, he was dead.'

It's a year or so since Julia's husband died, and she's still a relatively young woman – only in her mid-fifties. She says she has a lovely new home in Cork, which she and her husband had moved into just three months before he died. That's important, she says, because it doesn't hold a lifetime of memories and she can start again in the home and not feel weighed down by images of the past all around her. Although she's keen to say that she has no interest in meeting someone new or starting another relationship. She's heard all the clichés about grief and grieving from well-meaning people since her husband died. The biggest one of these is the phrase 'time is a healer'. 'It is,' she says, 'but you have to put in the time to heal. That's the hard bit they don't tell you about.'

Running Up That Hill

The chair had been sold to a man in west Cork, who had a heart procedure coming up and was nervous about the impact it might have on his mobility. He was sounding very pessimistic on the phone when they were organising collection and she says he was full of trepidation about what lay ahead. 'I'll bet,' Julia says, 'that he's had his operation and has made a great recovery and doesn't need the chair at all. I'll bet he's alive and kicking and will be for a long time to come and the chair is gathering dust somewhere, waiting for the next person to inhabit it.'

Part Three
PETS' CORNER

A MONKEY IS FOR LIFE – NOT JUST FOR CHRISTMAS

For sale: pair of breeding monkeys (with or without cage). *Evening Echo, 2014*

The above advertisement appeared in the pet pages of the *Evening Echo* among the birdcages, goldfish bowls, free kittens and pedigree puppies, during Christmas 2014. When I phoned the contact number, a man with a strong rural accent told me the monkeys were gone. He wasn't keen to go into the story of where the monkeys had come from or how he had come to possess them, but he did agree to put me in touch with the buyer. So the next morning I arrived at Rumley's Pet Farm, a few kilometres outside Cork city. Ivan Rumley told me that he'd already sold the male monkey but would be happy to show me around his mini-zoo and introduce me to the female.

This land had been earmarked for development during the boom (the last one, not the supposed

The Personals

current one), but the plans were never realised, and so now the Rumleys have done a great job building on their strategic position between Cork and Kerry to develop a tourist and educational business. And that's where the monkeys came in.

In one of the outhouses at the back of the farmhouse are two large pens, and inside one was a marmoset monkey, one of the smallest breeds in the world. 'She is just three years old and it was my first time seeing an advertisement for monkeys in the *Evening Echo*,' Ivan Rumley told me. The seller had bought them as pets from a dealer in Northern Ireland. It's easier to buy exotic animals on the island of Ireland than it is to buy a dog or a cat because of the lack of regulation. When the owner of the monkeys fell ill, he needed to offload them in a hurry and turned to the small ads. Ivan Rumley bought the pair for more than €1,000. 'To be honest, I was only looking in the *Echo* for a pony,' he told me.

FINDING SHANGRI-LA

> **Wanted by pensioner** – medium-sized mixed breed dog m/f for company and lots of country walks. Free to good home assured. *Evening Echo, July 2018*

Over the years I've been reading them, pensioners have posted some of the best and quirkiest ads I've come across. For example, a guy I rang one time was looking for a transistor radio. When I phoned him and we got talking, he told me he was about to start a campaign to get the city authorities to increase the height of all the bridges in Cork because he claimed swans were hitting their heads when they flew under them on their way to Canada ...

When I saw the above ad it drew me in straight away and thankfully the man behind it needed little persuading to tell me some of his story. We arranged to meet near Collins Barracks on the north side of

The Personals

Cork city. He was wearing colourful shorts and a Michael Jackson T-shirt. I reckoned he was in his sixties, but he could have been older. He was a tall man who pointed to a hearing aid in one ear, which meant I had to stand on his right-hand side so he could hear me properly. As we strolled to his house he was happy to chat about his life and particularly his attachment to dogs.

Before we met, he had given me the name of his estate, and because I had arrived early, I walked around wondering which house was his and whether I could match the voice to his physical space. One small bungalow with flowers growing from all angles outside and a bowl for a dog in the porch (bit of a giveaway) seemed a fairly strong possibility.

In the end, we didn't go as far as the house; he preferred to talk in my parked car outside his estate, although he struggled to get into it because of some ulcers on his leg that had just been dressed. Whenever possible, I prefer to meet people in their homes. It's their own patch, where they're usually most at ease and I'm the one out of my comfort zone a little, which helps balance the situation. The car works fine though, once people overcome their initial self-consciousness about a microphone being pointed towards them in a confined space.

I began, as I nearly always do, by asking Charlie to read out his ad for me, which he did in a lovely mellow

Finding Shangri-La

Cork voice, which had a tone perfectly befitting a man of his years. After he'd read the ad he started talking about his love of dogs and walking. 'I used to have three or four dogs all the time and I have lots of photographs at home of every place we walked – Carrignavar, Whitechurch, Rathpeacon and Glenbeigh,' Charlie told me. 'I don't walk for fitness. I just do it with the dogs. Any of the walks would be 10km out and 10km back. To be honest, that would be the shortest one I'd do.'

'And you wouldn't walk without the dogs?' I ask him. 'No, I did a few walks on my own there recently, that's why I advertised – 'twasn't the same thing, you see. The old dog I had wouldn't go out at all towards the end. He was fit enough, but he just wouldn't leave the estate. You'd miss the company,' he says.

Charlie has had dogs since he was 20, so for about half a century he's always had a canine companion. 'The first dog I adopted was out in Africa, in the Congo. I was in the army at the time and I was 18,' he explains. 'We were one of the last battalions to go out, the 38th, and there were always a few dogs around the camp. You weren't supposed to touch them in case of rabies, but there was a lovely young Alsatian that I got attached to. That was the first one I had, and then I used to look after a few in the barracks as there was always a couple of strays. And then people over the years gave me dogs, so I never really paid for any of them.'

The Personals

We talk about breeds that are suitable as family pets, which dogs work well in cities and the different temperaments of various breeds. When I ask which had been his favourite dog, his voice begins to crack with emotion and his eyes redden. He looks away from me out of the window, not wanting me to see him upset. He coughs, to borrow a line from Heaney, angry tearless sighs. 'I think ... the fella that died recently,' he says. 'He was a good-sized dog, like an Alsatian face. I had him 12 years and he got leukaemia two years ago and in two months he was gone.'

Was that loss hard to get over? ''Twas, yeah. I was in hospital at the time, because something went wrong with my heart. And I was in there a few days and the dog was on his last legs – he only got really bad the final week. They wouldn't leave me out of hospital. There were a few neighbours who looked after things. He died by the front door inside and he was dead when I came back.'

'You didn't get to say goodbye?'

'You're making me all emotional now,' he says, fighting back the tears. 'I took him down the ring road on a Sunday and I buried him near the fire station. I dug a hole for him down there.'

'Did you say a prayer?' I ask.

'No, I drank a bottle of wine though. I'm not religious at all. I'm after paying for a pre-funeral cremation for myself whenever I go. I told them to take the cross off the coffin and there'd be no priest involved.'

In any interview there are signposts to someone's past, departure points through which if someone is open enough, you can enter. This was an obvious one. I ask Charlie some more about this, because I assume he was raised a Catholic, so why the deliberate efforts to ensure that his funeral will have no religious element?

'I have three sisters and they are all married,' he tells me. 'They were all brought up in care. Just like me. Our mother was in a laundry, or county home as it was known then. And she was there till the day she died. And then I was sent to a convent in Cappoquin, and then when I was eight or nine I was sent to St Joseph's Industrial School. That was one of the most notorious ones. I wasn't assaulted. Well, physically, I was, but nothing else.'

I've interviewed survivors of industrial schools a few times over the years, and some of them, particularly those who decided not to seek redress afterwards, downplay their experiences. Some can't bear to face that painful aspect of their lives and therefore suppress what must have been a horrendous, loveless childhood. His mother remained a distant figure throughout his life.

'We never knew her,' he tells me. 'She was in a home all her life and was institutionalised. You couldn't really talk to her. I wanted to find out who my father was. On the birth certs there is no father's name and for my three sisters, it's the same.'

He doesn't know much about his family, except that they seemed to travel around a lot and never really had a place to call home. He remains in contact with his sisters and they have unearthed some information. He thinks his grandfather was killed during the Second World War, and his grandmother may also have spent time in a county home.

On several occasions during his childhood he was taken to see his mother, or she would come and see him, accompanied by his grandmother. These were difficult and often uncomfortable visits. 'We would be brought into a room in the convent,' he says. 'They would bring her down and we could talk to her for a while. She wouldn't say anything. Again, I would be trying to ask her questions about the history of the family and she wouldn't say a word. My mother was described as a domestic on my birth cert. Of course, I always wanted to know who fathered the four children, because I do know we weren't all the same father. I was seven years old before the next child was born. And then there was another four to five years till the third one and the same with the final one. It couldn't be the same person, as she was in a home all that time and had very little freedom, so we don't know who it was. My sister said she was going to look on social media and try to make connections. I'm illiterate as regards computers so there isn't much I can do.'

When his mother died in the 1980s, the funeral was held on a Sunday and Charlie didn't attend. He says he was only told she'd died the day before her funeral and it was midwinter and the roads were bad, but some of his sisters went as they were living near her. She was still living in the institution when she died and the religious order made all the arrangements for the funeral. He doesn't visit the grave regularly.

Charlie is 74 next month and is not sure now if he will ever learn the truth about his mother or his biological father. 'There was never a mention of my family living anywhere. I never had a home. I know that the policy was to leave you with the mother for the first two years so I must have spent time with her then. After that I was put into care and that was it really until I got away in my late teens.'

Some years ago, one of the first reports I remember working on with survivors of religious and industrial schools was about a group of men who had been in an industrial school in Baltimore, west Cork. They were nicknamed the 'blue-legged boys' by locals, because they were always underdressed and underfed. Many had never spoken of their experiences, and I remember after broadcasting the report from a studio in Cork, when the red light went off I cried alone in the studio, having carried their stories, experiences and abuses around in my head for less than a week.

I can't imagine what it must be like to have to carry those experiences around for a lifetime. Since I've become a father again and have small children running around the house, survivors' testimonies have impacted on me more personally and profoundly than before. The one thing that always strikes me is that survivors talk about childhoods devoid of any compassion, humanity or kindness. Some of them never received a hug or a kind word until they got married.

'Nobody ever showed me any affection,' Charlie says. 'I find I am not able to do that myself either. I am too embarrassed. That's the way I was brought up. I keep to myself mostly.' Looking back, he says he has had a tough life, but he's not a person to talk about his feelings or emotions to anyone. He keeps all that bottled up inside.

He takes half a dozen old photos out of his pocket. I was expecting them to be pictures of his family maybe or his early years in the army. Instead, he wanted to show me photos of his dogs through the years, each of them with their own personality. It's easy to see how dogs became close companions for Charlie, having grown up not knowing who his father is, and not being able to communicate with an institutionalised mother.

'I joined the army from school,' he tells me. 'After I left the industrial school without an education, they

Finding Shangri-La

sent me to another boarding school, collecting cutlery mainly. This was in a place called Ballyfin, which is some fancy hotel now. I only lasted six months and I left. To be totally honest, I joined the army because I never had a home up to that point and there was no social welfare at the time. Like many of us, I joined because we got bed and board. If I look back, I didn't really particularly like it, but I spent 17 years in it and it did offer me some security.'

Since leaving the army, Charlie has lived within a few hundred metres of the barracks in Cork all his life, first in a bedsit and then renting a flat, before a landlord discovered he was keeping dogs and asked him to leave. He's now in a small council house and has been living there for well over a decade. It has a small garden out the back and the dogs have been happy there. At various times over the years he has had up to five dogs. Now he is left with just one, a small Terrier that a woman on the south side of the city gave him after she saw his advertisement. It's four years old, and he'd purposely looked for a dog that age.

'I kept the ad in because I was going to get another one for company for this fellow but I'm not so sure now. I would always have them as puppies. But I am 74 now; there's a possibility I could die first, before the dogs. That's why I got a four-year-old and not a pup. I wouldn't want to die before them. Most of them couldn't be rehomed. They're one-man dogs.'

The Personals

By taking such practical steps, Charlie is facing his mortality head-on. He has been in and out of hospital a lot, and recently fell and dislocated his shoulder, which has further limited his mobility. He cannot imagine a scenario in which his dogs would be put down after he is gone, and so he says he will take the ad down in a few days' time and he and the Terrier will live out their days in his small cottage.

Before I leave, I ask Charlie what his full name is, so I can put it in my records and I'm surprised when he tells me his name isn't Charlie at all. It's Michael. But everyone calls him Charlie. Why is that?

'When I came into the army the first time, I was skin and bones, having come from the industrial schools,' he tells me. 'There was a Mr World everyone knew at the time called Charles Atlas, who was a bodybuilder type man. So, as a form of bullying I suppose they all called me Charlie and the name stuck.'

Darkness was falling and our conversation ended. We had gone from talking about wanting to adopt a medium-sized dog, to conflict in the Congo, to growing up in an industrial school and having a sense of place. I helped Charlie out of the car, and he unwound his long legs on to the footpath, picked up his plastic bag full of groceries and walked to his little cottage within a stone's throw of the military barracks. It turns out that it was the one with the dog bowl outside that I'd spotted earlier. He lives there, alone, but content.

He waved as a neighbour stopped him at his doorway for a chat. He seemed well placed in the area. The man who had had no place to call home for much of his life was now part of a community, had a front door key and was taken care of. This community were as much his family as his sisters, his institutionalised mother and the father he'd never known. To the right of his doorway on the wall of his home is a sign with the name of the house. The writing is a little faded and hard to read. The light was declining so I got closer to it and smiled as I made out the words.

It read: Shangri-La. An earthly paradise indeed.

MAKING IT PIG IN HOLLYWOOD

> **Four-year-old pair of Sandyspot pigs for sale.** Very quiet and tame, been on film sets for last 3½ years. Quick sale due to space needed. €200 the pair ono. ***DoneDeal, October 2018***

I'm at an animal reserve of sorts in County Wicklow to interview two pigs that starred in the *Game of Thrones* series. Become a journalist – travel the world, they said ...

The house is up a steep hill, and was clearly a farm at one point in time. Now it comprises two buildings spread across several hectares within a stone's throw of a dual carriageway. I park at the bottom of the hill, beside a Ford Focus with half of one side of its body crumpled up like wastepaper. I had visions of a rogue pig having channelled its inner Conor McGregor, running amok and destroying the car. Less dramatically,

Making It Pig in Hollywood

I later learn that a van with a faulty handbrake had rolled down the hill and caused the damage.

Let me set the somewhat surreal scene for you: a large, intimidating Alsatian is doing everything he can to break out of a cage and get to know me better as I walk through the yard. Given his eagerness to show me all his teeth at once, I doubt he wants to use me for licking practice. Next to him is an enormous raven in a cage, and next to the raven there are three monkeys. I can hear pigs in the distance, and there's a constant din of bird noises coming from one of the buildings. Think *Apocalypse Now*.

I'm early so I hang around admiring a cockatoo, then a jeep pulls into the yard and Eddie Drew gets out and offers me a friendly and firm handshake. 'I'm just on a break from the film set so I have about half an hour,' he tells me. 'Do you want to see the star pigs?'

How Eddie Drew came to own this prime property just off junction 8 in County Wicklow is a story in itself. This parcel of land with a farmhouse was originally owned by two elderly unmarried sisters, who had started an organic farm here decades before. 'I inherited this farm 30 years ago from the two old ladies who were making natural yoghurt here – the Miss Bakers I called them – they had a herd of 50 goats and they were way ahead of their time. I worked for them since I was young. They were organic and homeopathic and both happened to be spinsters and they supplied all the shops with home-made yoghurt.'

Eddie was left the farm of 30 acres, some of which he sold to pay inheritance tax. He says he knew after three or four years of working with the women that the property and land would be left to him and he is very grateful for that and feels a sense of responsibility for it.

His experience with animals up to that point had mainly involved horse riding lessons, but when he took on the farm, he stopped the yoghurt production as it had become too hard to compete with industrial producers, and instead he opened an aviary and a small pet shop. Then he began supplying animals for films being made in Ireland, beginning with *Braveheart* and continuing to the present day. Often he'll be asked to provide animals to dress a particular scene, such as a goat here or a raven there. And sometimes an animal

Making It Pig in Hollywood

is a more integral part of the film and has to be trained for the role.

The ad that brought me here is for two large pigs bought six years ago, who are possibly the most famous pigs in Ireland. They'd just come off the set of *Vikings*, having also starred in two seasons of the US series *Into the Badlands*. I half-expected them to emerge from their own trailer, Hollywood-style, with a team of bodyguards and PR handlers fussing around weeding out the blue M&M's, as requested. Instead, the 90kg male walked up to me, snorted into the microphone like a total pro, and went on his way again. And the reason Eddie is selling them now?

'I just picked up a bunch of wild boar down in Macroom,' he tells me. 'The *Vikings* wanted North American animals because it's moving location in terms of the script. So I now have a family of wild boars.'

Eddie is the kind of guy who can make or break an animal's showbiz career. Think of him as the Simon Cowell of the pig acting world. He tells me that the secret to having a happy pig on set is plenty of food and being nice to the animals. But good-tempered and professional as the pigs are, not all the actors they work with are good with animals.

'One of the best actors I ever worked with was Brendan Gleeson on a film called *Calvary*, where he played a priest,' Eddie tells me. 'He had a Golden

The Personals

Retriever in the film. We were down in Sligo and he really enjoyed working with the dog. Some of the Americans have never been around animals and are not hands-on. Brendan was a really hands-on guy. There was a scene where the dog had to lie in the bed and Brendan curled up beside the dog and was tickling his belly and they bonded brilliantly.'

The animals he provides aren't always as cuddly though. Eddie tells me of a scene two years ago for which he had to provide a pit of 75 snakes for a character who was killed off. 'We were up in the Sally Gap and had to dig this pit and put the snakes in and the actor was lowered into it in a cage. Another time we had 150 rats out on the set of *Penny Dreadful* and we also had to teach a character how to skin a dead rabbit.'

Eddie even ended up in *Vikings* himself, playing the Norse god Odin in seasons one and three. He says that the movie business is very tedious work, with actors having to do take after take until a director is happy. Many of the animals on his farm are either for sale or rent and most have acting experience. A pig will cost a film €100 a day, for example. He keeps three squirrel monkeys as pets, and has had them and their parents for over 20 years, and he also has pet rats, magpies, snakes and ravens.

The ad has been up a week and so far he's had only one call, from a neighbour, it turns out. 'He wanted

Making It Pig in Hollywood

them for meat and I told him where to go,' Eddie says. 'If someone buys them for that, fair enough, but I'm not going to sell them if I know that's where they're going to go.'

And the hardest animals that he has worked with so far? 'Humans, all day long,' he says.

Part Four
ARTICLES OF WAR

MARRIED TO THE PAST

For sale: genuine Nazi flag and First World War helmet. *DoneDeal, November 2016*

There's quite a lot of historical memorabilia for sale on sites such as DoneDeal and you see the odd item in the classified sections of newspapers too. Mainly they're posted because a relative has died and a family member is clearing the house or settling the estate and finds they have to sell war medals or memorabilia.

This ad in November 2016 was fairly unusual, in that a person was selling a Second World War Nazi flag, which I hadn't seen before, and a First World War helmet, which is somewhat rarer. The flag was branded and marked as a genuine flag and complete with large swastika. There's a debate to be had about whether these kinds of items should be sold at all, and whether allowing a secondary market to exist risks

The Personals

romanticising one of the most efficient murdering machines in history. And there's always the chance that these items might fall into the wrong hands.

I went to meet the seller and as often happens, I found myself parked in a garage forecourt beside a car wash, trying to spot a stranger among the customers going in and out. He was very clear that he didn't want me going to his home, for reasons that would later emerge. He was in his late thirties, a working man with a young family and into fitness – mostly cycling. Once he was sitting in the car, I decided to jump straight in and began by asking him how someone comes to own a genuine Nazi flag.

'A few years back I was working in Holland and there was an auction,' he told me. 'I picked it up there and brought it home. It supposedly came from a house clearance, same as it would do in Ireland. It's part of their complicated history and I think at the time I paid around €120 for it.'

I had hoped to see the flag, but he told me that wasn't possible because he had sold it the previous day. He'd had it up online for a few weeks and there had been sporadic interest, but the person who'd bought it was a collector. What's interesting is that for the most part these items can be sold in Ireland, but you probably couldn't put this up on eBay, or sell it in many parts of Europe because of legislation banning the sale of Nazi-themed items. Does he think that

Married to the Past

through allowing a secondary market to develop for these items some level of glorification and justification will follow?

He disagrees, and the way he sees it is that he'd had a chance to buy a slice of history and he took it. As we sat in the car he opened a plastic bag and handed me the helmet, which had once sat on the head of a German soldier during the First World War. 'You don't see too many of these any more,' he told me, as he tossed the great hulk of steel to me. The weight of it took me by surprise, as I held several kilos of heavy German engineering in my lap. 'The Germans were known for their great steel, and this helmet was way ahead of the helmets at the time,' he said.

So how much would this cost me if I wanted an early Christmas present for my wife? 'World War One. German. I would say you'd be looking at €200 to €250,' he replied. I think I'll just stick to vouchers for bath products from Lush, I tell him.

Given this man's passion, I was half-expecting him to tell me that the item had pride of place in his living room, in a purpose-built cabinet maybe, just under the Sacred Heart and above the photo of Jack Charlton. He had remained tight-lipped about his name and address, and didn't want to go into any details that might identify him. I assumed this was because he had a huge collection of valuable items and was worried about break-ins.

The Personals

The truth was that his wife didn't know he had the items. 'Everything ends up in the shed,' he explained. 'Since I was married, I couldn't keep this kind of stuff in my bedroom any more as the wife wanted nothing to do with it. She doesn't want it in the house. So anything I buy or sell along these lines goes into the shed and she usually doesn't see any of it.'

I've established that this man isn't a neo-Nazi or far right type, unlike many I've met over the years. The thrill for him is simply a link to history that he can own and share. Except in his case he mostly shares it with himself in his garden shed, away from the disapproving eyes of his nearest and dearest. Now he's married, like a lot of us, his life has to change somewhat. For some, that means cutting down on golfing days away or weekends on the beer. It might mean adding a few extra centimetres to your waist or wearing matching pyjama sets. For him, being married means off loading the Nazi items in the shed. There's naught as funny as folk, as the saying goes.

'GROW WHEAT – THE CROP THAT PAYS'

Vintage Second World War propaganda poster. €240. *DoneDeal, July 2018*

Today, Wexford's Main Street is unrecognisable when compared to the time O'Connor's shop was a stable presence there, from the early part of the twentieth century until it closed in the 1970s. The family still owns the building where the shop was, and during its heyday it sold everything from hardware to groceries. These days, as a sign of changing consumer trends, it's a mobile phone accessories store.

Some people say if you want to see how much society has evolved over the past century, you need look no further than our main streets. Cafes are replacing bars, flat whites are the new half pints, while 'convenience' and 'express' are the buzzwords for shops. Online shopping will change the streets even further in the coming decades, as more and more of us

The Personals

decide it's not worth the hassle or time to leave the house to shop.

The daughter of the owner of O'Connor's is Helen Duggan, and she lives in the family homestead of Carcur House in Wexford. It's a beautiful old Georgian property with a rich history, and is appropriately filled with antique furniture and naval artefacts brought back from trips abroad by several generations of sailors in the family.

The propaganda poster advertised was such an unusual item that I had to go and meet Helen. On the face of it, it's a simple enough poster, which at one time hung in the shop window of P. J. O'Connor and Sons in Wexford town. The ad originally said it was a First World War poster dated 1917, but further investigation found that it was issued and hung during the middle years of the Second World War.

Helen leads me to the sunroom, where she has an assortment of items laid out on the table, from ration books to old shop advertisements and ledgers. We have tea and home-made lemon cake, and she begins to tell me a bit about herself and her family. 'I was born and reared here and very much involved in local history. The house is several centuries old, and it has character. As they say, houses like this own you, you don't own them,' says Helen, pouring the freshly-made tea.

I say I imagine that when you go up into the attic of an old house like this, it's like entering Aladdin's Cave.

'Grow Wheat – The Crop That Pays'

'Don't go there,' she says, 'I'm a third-generation hoarder. I've been systematically working through each room and trying to catalogue everything. My grandfather started a business and before that my family were all seafarers, and a lot of the men were lost at sea. So my grandfather wasn't allowed to go to sea, which he was very disappointed about, so then he started a hardware business.' Dotted around the house are shells that her great-grandfather brought back from overseas, as well as prints of the ships the family worked on over the years.

In the middle of the table was the poster, with the words 'Grow Wheat – The Crop that Pays' written large on it. It was probably about A3 size, with colours as vibrant as if it had come off the printing press yesterday, not eight decades previously as was the case. 'This is something we found out in the coach house in a pile of rubble and dust,' Helen tells me. 'It's a poster which was to encourage the growing of wheat during the Emergency, as it was called. It hung on the front window of the commercial premises on Main Street and it's signed by a man called W. Till. Seemingly he was asked by the government to produce a poster for this. He was one of the well-known artists behind these at the time. Bar one I saw in Irish online, it is fairly rare to see these. A lot of them were just thrown away.'

Looking more closely at the poster, I can't help but notice a significant hole in the middle fold about the

The Personals

size of a €2 coin, with accompanying frayed edges. Maybe an overenthusiastic shop assistant had tugged it off the window? 'No, unfortunately the result of a lovely little mouse, we think,' Helen says. 'It's a good job he got full and didn't keep going.'

Now comes the *Antiques Roadshow* moment, when I pause before asking if she has any idea what it is currently worth. 'Well, had it been intact I am advised it is worth €2,500. Because of the damage by that little mouse, it is somewhere in the hundreds now. Because we have done up the coach house, we're not too worried because if it doesn't sell, we'll just keep it there.'

The ad had been up a few weeks when we met, but so far, the interest hasn't been huge. 'It's a very specialised area,' she says. 'There's one man interested and he has a few thousand old ones, so we've been talking and we'll see where it goes.'

O'Connor's shop was on Main Street from the late 1920s. Although it's rented out, the family try to preserve the shop front as it should be, in an effort to stay loyal to the past. Talking to Helen it's clear that the link with history and the commercial life that once existed is becoming more difficult to assert. And while Main Street has always evolved, it does seem that there's been a more dramatic and significant shift in the last few years than in the previous decades.

Also in the collection of items related to the shop that Helen discovered in the coach house were ration

'Grow Wheat – The Crop That Pays'

books, petrol coupons and old credit ledgers. They provide a fascinating insight into the days of credit, a time when some farmers paid their accounts once a year at harvest time. It also details those customers who never settled, who still have amounts outstanding decades later. Shops like O'Connor's were so embedded in their communities, I'd imagine it was difficult to call in the bailiffs when someone couldn't or wouldn't pay. Helen remembers calling at some houses looking for payment, but it was a pointless exercise. This was the late seventies and many simply didn't have the money and so their outstanding amounts remain frozen in time.

Since the coach house has been cleared, Helen says her husband allows her two sections to clutter to her heart's content. We take a walk outside and into the beautiful original coach house, just metres from the back door. Helen shows me some great finds, not least of which is a collection of chimney lamps, as well as lots of boating items and antique furniture.

The family tells a story that one night more than a century ago there was a party in the house. The owners had a tip-off that there would be a police raid later that night. Family members dropped a cache of pistols and swords into a well. Some time later, a group slipped in while the party was in full swing and took many of the items from the well, except for one French bayonet, which the family retains and displays proudly.

The Personals

While the coach house has now been cleared of decades worth of gathered items, and many of them will be put up online for sale, given Helen's passion for collecting, I doubt the space will remain decluttered for long. She waves me off, telling me to ignore the large panels of ornate conservatory glass leaning against the side of her house. 'They're beautiful,' I say, as I pause to lift some of the panels and look at the detail. 'Yes, they are,' she says, 'We believe they came from a house with links to the Duke of Wellington. The whole conservatory is there. Someday I'll assemble it. I'd like nothing better than to put it back like it once was and restore it to what it looked like in its heyday – give it a new lease of life.'

ZEN AND THE ART OF PHONE BOX MAINTENANCE

For sale: Second World War German military helmet in great condition. Complete with lining and strap. Belonged to Nazi firefighter. €90. *DoneDeal, August 2018*

The taxi drops me off halfway up Collins Avenue in Dublin, where I'm met at the door by fifty-something Paul Murphy who, it turns out, is a somewhat unlikely collector of a wide range of unusual items.

In his sitting room and hallway are about a dozen grandfather clocks at various stages of restoration, while an oversized vintage squash racket and a small model of an old phone box sit on a kitchen shelf. Paul describes himself as a collector and part-time seller and he can trace his collecting roots back to childhood, when he was fascinated by stamps and built up a sizeable collection.

The Personals

He began putting ads online about 12 years ago, he tells me, when his passion was ignited by old clocks. It started casually enough; he became interested after buying one or two randomly at car boot sales and restoring them. He'd bring them back to life and put them on the mantelpiece and over time he ended up with too many. And like any collector who has too many things, he inevitably became a part-time dealer.

As I've been finding out from the collectors I meet through the small ads, the pathways to building up collections are not exactly casual. And so it was with Paul. He became focused on collecting certain types of items at a time in his life when his mental health was suffering. Restoring old pieces of furniture or items of historical significance became vital therapy for him, and allowed him to work through issues in a structured way. It began with an old phone box which he bought and put in the front garden.

'I love the old Irish phone boxes and you don't see them on the ads that often, but a few years ago one came up on DoneDeal,' he explains. 'We were in west Cork for the weekend. I had a very big job in security but I suffered from depression and anxiety at the time so I had taken a break from the job and I was out of work. So anyway, I saw this old phone box. It was in bits, but myself and the owner did a deal, and I went and collected it on the Tuesday morning after our weekend away. It was great therapy. I couldn't get it into the back garden; because it is solid concrete it weighs about two tonnes, so I put it out the front. I owe that first phone box a hell of a lot.'

Paul was born in 1964 and as a teenager in the late 1970s and 1980s, he was intimately familiar with the inside of phone boxes. He felt huge nostalgia towards the phone box, and he set about restoring it to its original condition, working on it in his front garden daily for about two months. 'Every day I was there working on it, at least four or five people would stop and talk to me about their memories; what went on in them, and their recollections of the glass being replaced and how they fiddled the phones and stuck paper up the coin return,' he says.

The work became daily therapy for Paul and was a way of keeping his mind and body engaged in a task. It also helped to keep at bay the isolation and social withdrawal that often comes with a period of poor mental health. 'My wife saw the value in it from day one,' he says. 'That's why there was never any hassle having it out the front. I used to have the door of the phone box in the kitchen and other bits of it all over the sitting room. My wife saw it as a huge positive because it prevented me from sitting inside watching TV all day long and staying in my head.'

It's difficult for Paul to pinpoint exactly where his depression came from or what the trigger was. 'It's hard to know,' he says. 'I do think my excessive drinking was as a result of self-medicating with alcohol for depression. But then alcohol of course is a depressant, so it is a vicious circle. I went off drink around this time, and the energy I used to put into drinking now goes into restoration and into antiques.'

I asked Paul to describe depression to someone who may have no idea what it is. 'It's just the weight of the world on you when it shouldn't be and things get blown up out of proportion,' he says. 'The flipside is when you're doing something like restoring a phone box; it gives a lot back and you can see the benefit.'

Paul says it's not an exaggeration to claim that replying to the phone box ad on DoneDeal probably saved his life, in terms of helping him work through his mental health issues, keeping the depression at bay and preventing it from escalating. In the years since, he's been buying and selling things on DoneDeal and various other sites on a weekly basis. He recently got rid of a lot of items he had gathered over the years and made a few quid in the process. That decluttering exercise only means one thing – now he can start cluttering and collecting all over again.

Zen and the Art of Phone Box Maintenance

Which brings us to his current ad, for a German Second World War firefighter's helmet, which along with a few other items was found on a weekend break in Berlin with his wife. I'm jealous. When my wife and I went to Berlin one November a few years ago all we came back with were head colds and we spent our weekend drifting from coffee shop to coffee shop, trying to keep frostbite at bay. Paul picked up a holster belonging to a German soldier, an oversized squash racket and some German bar signs. Thinking of the baggage charges, I sincerely hope he didn't travel Ryanair.

'The holster is for a Walther PPK 7.65,' he tells me, handing me a small leather pouch. 'It is German and

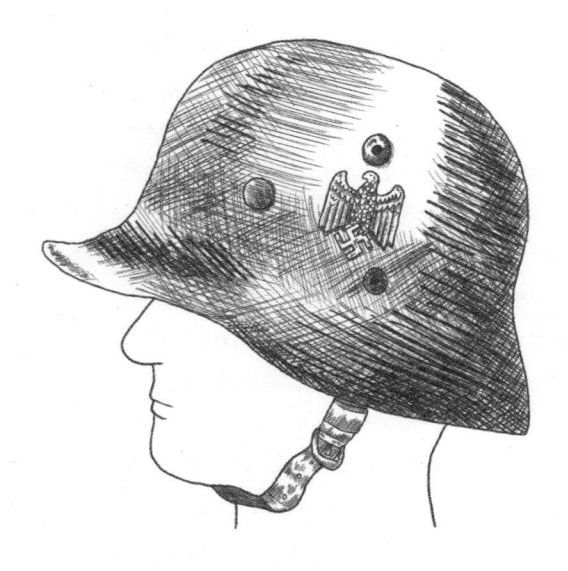

The Personals

has the stamp saying 1941 on it and the eagle crest. That's a nice little piece. The helmet I got in Berlin a few weeks ago too. We went over with just two carry-on cases in luggage and then we bought two huge suitcases over there and paid the charges coming back. This helmet has the year 1939 stamped on it and the regiment on it too, so I need to look into that a bit more and find out more about it.'

Like many I've met who are enthused by military items, Paul is drawn to military memorabilia because of the stories behind them, both personal and political. 'The war is so emotive,' he says, 'You look at these items, and I think of the soldier in 1939 that had it on him, with stuff flying everywhere. That was a German soldier out there conquering Poland or doing God knows what kind of evil – it beggars belief to be so close to history, to have it in your hand.'

No one has answered his ad so far, but he expects a lot of interest given the historical heritage. I have a nose around the other pieces littering his kitchen and sitting room floor. It's such an eclectic range of items, and the collection is led by curiosity rather than having any overarching theme. For example, Paul shows me a pile of small pieces of parquet flooring that look slightly charred, neatly stacked in mounds lining the hallway. You have to step round them to access the kitchen. There are about 20 pieces stacked against the wall, and some are slotted together like jigsaw

Zen and the Art of Phone Box Maintenance

pieces, with others on their own waiting for a mate. 'This is my next project,' he tells me. 'It's a floor I bought from an old school in England, and I'm going to put it down in the sitting room. Each little piece has to be treated and then fitted. It will take months to clean, assemble and lay the floor but in the end it will be worth it.'

This means hard physical work ahead, but more importantly for Paul, these will be months when his mind is kept busy. Thankfully, since he stopped drinking alcohol and began restoring more items, the temptation to get drunk has left him. People find zen through all sorts of things – for some it's restoring an old car, for others it's ruining a good walk on a golf course. Paul gets it through the classifieds and they give him more than months of counselling or medication could. They give him a purpose and a wide social network to engage with, meaning he remains connected and valued. Having fully restored three phone boxes and a huge amount of collected material, he hasn't had an episode of depression in years. Life is good. 'And all this because I answered an ad online,' he says.

ENGINEERING A STEP BACK IN TIME

First World War relics from Verdun, France, 1917. Original consists of 2 French Grenadier uniform buttons, one shaped bullet and an 1870 French Third Republic medal. €40. ***DoneDeal, October 2018***

The odds that Michael Daly would become an engineering and technical graphics teacher were fairly slim. Pretty much all his family, including his father, left school early and took the boat to England after the Second World War. There was little work in Ireland and a lot of rebuilding to be done on the other side of the Irish Sea.

Michael went down a different path and was always single-minded in his choices. For example, after his Inter Cert he wanted to drop woodwork and study history, which at that time wasn't available in his school. His principal forbade it, but Michael did it anyway, finding a history teacher nearby and spending his Saturday mornings going through the curriculum. In the end he got good marks in both subjects and went on to train as a teacher, becoming the first in his family to go to university. He is still teaching today, not far from his home in Ardagh. We meet in a hotel in Newcastle West after his working day and he brings with him two boxes of items he thinks will interest me, all with historical or cultural significance.

Michael's love of history came primarily from his father, who left Ireland when he was young. 'He was really interested in buying and selling over the years,' Michael says. 'In fact, some of the stuff I'm going to show you here came from him, and was sourced in London when he was working there. He went there in the sixties and he'd be home maybe three or four weeks of the year and I would go over to him on my holidays.'

This situation was often referred to as an Irish divorce, when Irish men went away to work and came back for very short periods of time. Michael says his mother didn't like London, and couldn't stand the hustle and the bustle. During all those years she kept things going at home, balancing three kids while working two jobs. His father sent money home every few weeks, and she passed away before he retired, so they never spent 52 weeks of the year together again after he emigrated.

The Personals

He did come home for her funeral. 'She's dead 20 years now,' Michael says. 'My father is dead seven years, and when he died, there was a shed load of stuff left.'

Every school holiday Michael had joined his father in London and worked on the building sites. His father did groundwork mainly, messy stuff Michael calls it, such as laying foundations and block paving. He did quite well at one stage, becoming a small sub-contractor and he worked with the large builders McAlpines, but was eventually squeezed out by the bigger players.

When Michael joined his father in London he also worked in construction, and this continued until the first few years he was teaching, before he got married. He describes his father as a typical 1960s Irish man, with drinking being one of his favourite pastimes. 'He drank and he played hard, but he worked hard then as well, and he worked till the day he retired. Then he came back home to Ireland to the family home.'

Michael's collecting had started when his father bought him a stamp album one Christmas when he was about 10 years old. From there he collected coins, and still does. When he was in London with his father they had a routine every Sunday which became important to his collecting. 'We used to go to a car boot sale in Hackney every Sunday morning and then we'd go a little bit down the road to a place called Brick Lane. We would do the markets until lunchtime and then

Engineering a Step Back in Time

we'd go for a few drinks in Mile End. We always bought something, so I was always collecting bits and pieces and would bring them home in the boot of a car, back on the ferry when it was time to leave.'

And with that, Michael opens the box on the table in front of him and starts taking out some of the items inside. He has several of them for sale online and others he has collected over the years. He shows me original bank receipts and invoices for a bridge built in Wales by McAlpines, dating back to the 1920s. These may not be worth much, he says, but they have special significance for him given his father's connection to McAlpines.

Sitting alongside these very British and London Irish items was a German soldier's book in immaculate condition. 'I was kind of always into military stuff,' he says. 'The uniforms and the ceremony look very well. This was an ordinary Wehrmacht soldier's from the Second World War. In 1944 the resources weren't there to do photographs, so there's a description of what he looks like written inside. This is like his passport, all stamped, showing everything from his vaccines to his gear kit. He survived, and we know this because his demobilisation papers are included here too. William Schmidt was his name: born in 1898, he was demobbed in 1946, so he probably spent time in a prisoner-of-war camp in Germany. I picked this up in Berlin a number of years ago when I was leading a school tour. I got it in an antiques shop. It's a fascinating slice of history and only cost me €50. It's not for sale though.'

Other items he shows me include deeds from the 1660s written on animal hide, a Victorian fan as well as various small buttons and medals from the First World War that he has for sale on DoneDeal. He also takes out a small hand pistol which he found on a building site in Hackney in the 1980s. 'It's a little one shot pistol and it's almost like a .22 – you put a bullet in and lock it into place,' he says, demonstrating how it works. 'The trigger and all is working. It's late 1800s, and it's German. I was digging on a work site and found it. I've a few Roman coins also that I got on sites. My uncle found a bag of them when he used to operate a digger. The pistol was all muck and dirt; it was something you would hold in your hand and conceal. It would have to be used at close range, with just one bullet. You'd make sure you were on target or else.'

While Michael is happy to offload some of his items, much of his collection he takes out and looks at regularly, unlike other collectors I've met. He had hoped his son might want to carry on the tradition of collecting that his father passed on to him. But this looks increasingly unlikely. 'My son is more interested in the Xbox or PlayStation than this stuff,' he says. 'I look at the online ads every single day. I look at my own ads, but also, I'm looking for specific things: Lady Lavery banknotes at the moment and an Iron Cross, 1st Class. You're always looking for something'

Continuing the collecting and carrying on a tradition his father introduced him to during those school holidays in London is a way of keeping his father present. We reflect on the Irish travelling to London today – putting down roots in areas such as Clapham Common and establishing GAA teams in places like Fulham. While close in physical proximity to the once thriving Irish communities in places such as Kilburn and Cricklewood, the current emigrant's experience of London couldn't be more different from the Irish who emigrated in the fifties and sixties. Their building sites are now tech hubs, while cheap Ryanair flights mean they're unlikely to be home just one week a year. It's more likely once a month now, leaving little room for the modern-day version of the Irish divorce of the past to continue.

Michael thinks he may leave the items in his collection to a local museum and what he doesn't want he will continue to sell on DoneDeal. One room in his home that was meant to be an office now houses the collection. He calls it his cubbyhole, and among the items on the wall is a US flag from the Kuwait War, which his brother, who served during the conflict, gave him. 'When I'm sitting in my room, I sometimes look around the walls. I'm surrounded by hundreds of years of war and I'm transported back to a moment in history,' he says. 'That's the real thrill for me.'

THE WEIGHT OF HISTORY

> **War of Independence medals for sale. Genuine provenance.** *DoneDeal,* ***September 2018***

It feels like the rain on the Isle of Man constantly has the wind egging it on, like a scrum half pushing his forwards into a ruck, so that when it hits you it does so with added intensity and pressure. It's an unusual place, where 70,000 or so people share a chunk of land in the Irish Sea just 13 miles from Liverpool. It's famous for a road race each year in which at least one participant nearly always dies, and for transforming itself from a holiday destination into a tax haven.

In some ways this change was necessary, as cheap continental flights from the 1970s onwards meant that the island could no longer rely on the hordes of UK tourists it had been receiving since the nineteenth century. Today, asset management, gambling and

The Weight of History

offshore investment companies have replaced the deckchairs and ice cream parlours of previous eras, and post Panama Papers there has been renewed focus on this semi-sovereign state.

As well as being a refuge for the tax shy, the island has also been a refuge of sorts for people who want to escape their past. Gerard Kelly is one of those people. He left his native Omagh for the first time when he was 15, taking the boat to England like tens of thousands of his contemporaries. Now in his early fifties, he tells me he's been living on the island for over a decade. Gerard had kindly offered to collect me from the small airport at one end of the island, when I arranged to meet him after seeing the medals he had advertised for sale online. On the journey to a coffee shop, in between swapping parenting stories and mortgage woes, he relayed something of a potted history of his upbringing in 1970s and 1980s Northern Ireland.

'I left Omagh first in 1988,' he tells me. 'There was no work there then. I remember the year only because I arrived in London the same month Ireland beat England in football. I remember picking up the papers and seeing the headline "Paddywhacked" and thinking, how can they even write that.'

The irony for Gerard and many of his neighbours in the 1970s and 1980s is that the very country that was making life difficult for them at home in Omagh, as they saw it, was also the one that offered them a

The Personals

way out. 'Yeah, that was strange for me because I left a garrison town with a British Army base,' Gerard says. 'There were a few small bombs but no major violence. You really became aware you were Catholic when you left school and found opportunities limited. You couldn't have got a job in the council or the water board, or anything like that because it was all Protestants. You'd get a job in the building site no bother, but you couldn't get decent money jobs. Nobody in my class went to university, for example.'

So Gerard set off for London with no money and little education. His first stop was the Holloway Road and the Cock Tavern. Through people he met there, the next day he was on a building site, working outside Battersea Dogs Home. His existence for the first few years became the clichéd pub-centred one which many Irish fell into abroad.

'You kept moving job to job. It was well paid but we were working for agencies and had to go to The Archway Tavern to get paid on a Friday,' he tells me. 'There was a wee boy in a hatch and they gave you a five-pound meal ticket and a pint while you were

The Weight of History

waiting for your money to be cashed. It was just a bar full of Paddies, but then everyone stayed there. The agency would take their money and the bar would take their money and there was a queue out the street of Irish people and everyone stayed on and drank. I always said the worst people to work for were my own. They treated you like shit because they knew there was another busload or planeload over in the morning. There was none of this Irish camaraderie. The worst thing about an Irishman is when they get money because they turn into totally different people. You might say that about everyone but it's something to do with the Irish; we're not suited to having a lot of money.'

Despite the unsympathetic attitude of his countrymen, Gerard was glad to be away from Northern Ireland and the Troubles. He knows that had he stayed his life would have been very different. It brings to mind a joke told about a fanatic IRA cell somewhere in west Clare and the accusation: 'Well, ye're not exactly on the frontline, lads.'

This works in reverse too. It's easy, particularly post 9/11, to be anti-Republican, or to judge those who got involved in the armed struggle from the safety of the Free State. Gerard is clear – had he stayed in Northern Ireland he too would have got involved. 'I would have been sucked in. I still have Republican tendencies but I definitely would have been involved some way or another. Thank God I didn't,' he says.

The Personals

'We were like Catholic ghettos. We never met a Protestant. I didn't meet a Protestant until I was about 18 years old and had been living away for a few years. Catholics stayed in Catholic areas. And then the Brits would come around your houses and you threw stones and petrol bombs at them. It was bad times. Going back to the days of Lloyd George and Churchill, the Brits always hated us. Some still do. Some still think we're all going around digging spuds up. I hate that fucking attitude.'

Gerard grew up in a world where people from the Republic of Ireland were called rednecks and Free Staters who had sold out his community. 'That was the mentality. To be honest, I still think that. A lot of people revere Michael Collins. He was bad to his own people though. He's not my hero,' he adds.

We've been talking for over half an hour by this stage, and haven't yet mentioned the medals he has for sale. After finishing our coffee Gerard suggests a trip around Douglas, the capital of the island, and we go for a spin. There's a real sense of faded grandeur about it. The curved white colonial terraces still look impressive, but behind them are poor-quality housing and the damaged signs of backstreet Indian takeaways come more and more into view.

Gerard spent a few years in London and then in the early 1990s decided to return home. By this stage he had developed a huge interest in music and the rave

The Weight of History

scene was about to take off. He was ahead of the curve and brought some of that music back with him from London. While people he knew in his area were going around shouting 'Up the RA' and painting Republican slogans on the walls, he was listening to The Specials and wearing braces. This didn't go down well with the local mini Devs.

'I was getting battered in my own housing estate,' he says. 'I remember one Christmas I got a cheap Walkman. I was going up through the housing estate and I got jumped. To go to the shop from my housing estate was like a war in itself. I had to go about two miles out of the way to go to the shop as I would get battered at the local shop because I wasn't going around shouting "Up the RA" every two minutes – instead I was listening to music.'

With the early rave scene came the drugs, namely ecstasy, and Gerard became as committed to them as he was to the beats. First, he took them himself, and then he later sold ecstasy to feed his own habit. 'It was escapism for me, from my life and my house at the time,' he says.

He says what was interesting about the early rave scene in Northern Ireland was that there wasn't the sectarian hatred inside the clubs that existed outside. Ecstasy eroded all that. 'Nobody bothered about religion in that scene. Everyone just went raving. You'd go out on a Friday night and you mightn't come home till

The Personals

Tuesday. Then you had the guys on the other side of town that hated you. The Provos. Or as we used to call them "armchair Provos". Boys sitting at the bar and shouting "Up the RA". They wanted to batter us too, so it was a them and us thing again. I always seemed to be fighting against somebody and not wanting to be.'

Initially, ecstasy got Gerard away from everything, but after a while the drugs also began wearing him down. He says he has about a dozen convictions, mostly for doing stupid things when drunk or high; some of them are for assaults on police officers. He wanted to go to America for his fiftieth birthday but couldn't get a visa, while recently he successfully secured a job as a postman, only to fail the police vetting. That hit him hard as he felt his past was weighing him down, following him around – stalking him almost.

When he first arrived on the Isle of Man he began taking cocaine. He was living in a flat and one Christmas he went to stay in a local hotel, drinking gin and playing a bit of golf. He says he remembers coming home on the Sunday and starting to feel this huge down. 'I was in the bathroom and I had a breakdown. I thought I can't be doing this any more. I'd been doing it for 10 years. I could never go into that bathroom again after that and I used to have to go into the leisure centre for a shower. So that was it for

The Weight of History

me then and aside from one or two slips, I've been off it for 10 years now.'

I can see why Gerard loves island life; it's another form of escapism. There is an island mentality that takes a while to get used to though. For example, some locals he knows have a saying: 'If you don't like it, there's a boat in the morning.' On one level, you're never fully accepted coming from the mainland, but that suits him. He's never quite fitted in anywhere anyway. It's a safe environment for the kids and a totally different kind of upbringing from the one he had in Northern Ireland during the Troubles.

He hasn't entirely cut his ties with his Republican past though, and he maintains an active interest in history, especially all things 1916. He rolls up his sleeve to proudly show me a Pádraig Pearse tattoo with the words: 'Éire Gan Saoirse. Éire Gan Síocháin' – meaning 'Ireland without freedom, Ireland without peace'. We talk about how complex Republicanism has become, particularly post 9/11, and how the bombing campaign on mainland Britain impacted on the many tens of thousands of Irish living there.

His interest in Republican tradition continued and it merged with his passion for online ads. His small time online buying and selling began a few years ago when he saw a fiftieth anniversary Pádraig Pearse coin for sale online and bought it. We're now in the office where he works. On the table is a box which he opens

The Personals

and takes out three medals related to the War of Independence.

'I never thought I'd get something like this,' he says, handing me the ribboned discs. He has a framed copy of the Proclamation in the hallway of his home and had been on the lookout for medals to hang off it. By chance, he saw these medals and had some spare money so he went for it. Soon after he bought them he put them up for sale online, but later grew attached to them, and has taken them down again since we spoke on the phone. He's determined to hold on to them, especially now he has done a bit of research into where the medals came from and who owned them.

'The guy I got them off told me they were belonging to his grandfather,' Gerard tells me. 'But I didn't believe it 100 per cent until I looked into it. I was worried whether they were going to be real or fake or what. Then he was telling me about his grandfather and I checked up on it. I couldn't believe it. I was able to put a face to the medals, an actual human being, and now I'm obsessed with finding out more about him and his fight for freedom.'

He says while he'd like to leave the medals to his own son one day, he doesn't want him to inherit any hang-ups about the Troubles. 'I don't even want him to be playing rebel songs,' he says. 'Why should another generation be burdened with that? I felt kind of strange buying something so personal from the

The Weight of History

grandson of the man who was awarded them. So the other day I texted the guy I bought them from and told him I would give him first option to buy them back. He said no thanks, and told me they'd been lying in a press for 50 years. I could sell them if I wanted and have a nice holiday, but after I'd come back, I'd have nothing to show. To be honest, I don't think I'd ever get rid of them now.'

*

The story behind the medals takes me from the Isle of Man to the west coast of Ireland, where a man named Peter had heard rumours when he was growing up about his grandfather's past, but he says, as in many families, it wasn't something that was spoken about often. If it was discussed, children were certainly never present.

He knew for example that his grandfather had lost half of one of his fingers when he was in an internment camp called Ballykinlar. He was also aware that his grandfather had remained an unapologetic Republican until his death in 1977, but apart from that, his grandfather never spoke directly to him about his early life. 'From what I can gather, when families got together at Christmas or came home from England, the adults talked about the past,' Peter tells me. 'Most of my grandfather's children moved to

The Personals

England to work and my father was the only one that stayed here in Ireland. My father came from a big family and he is 83 years old now, but most of his siblings are dead.'

Even when his aunts and uncles were alive, Peter doesn't ever remember a big family discussion about their father and his past. The one inescapable link was the medals as well as an old diary which was locked in a press for the best part of 50 years. Through them, Peter came to know that his grandfather, Jack, from Tubbercurry, County Sligo, had been an active member of the IRA in the 1920s. He was interned at Ballykinlar Prison Camp in 1921 with about 1,000 others. He knows that his grandfather's autograph book contains the signatures of some active IRA members. One of them, he says, was a well-known attempted escapee who was shot while trying to escape, and there's some suggestion that Eamon de Valera signed the diary, though he hasn't been able to locate his signature.

Peter doesn't know how the family came to be on the Republican side in the War of Independence. He doesn't know much about his great-grandparents either. Their surname, which he prefers to keep private, is from the Sligo area. He thinks maybe there are Hungarian connections somewhere along the line. He knows that many of the family were anti-treaty and their Republicanism has carried on to the present

The Weight of History

generation. Peter and his father attended the Easter Rising commemoration most years, and living quite close to the border, they remain steadfast in their belief that a united Ireland is possible.

'A lot of my father's friends would have been active,' he says. 'I remember cards being played in the house and a lot of well-known Republican Tubercurry names involved. As for my grandfather, he must have been very active, but what he was doing exactly, I don't know. He was up to something and interned for it. I know his job outside of the IRA would have been as a lorry driver and working in transport. Maybe that's a clue to what he did in the IRA at a time when there was a lot of guns being moved about.'

Peter's grandfather received an IRA pension in later life, but he says he has found it difficult to find out much about his service. One of his medals is for active duty, but he thinks his grandfather, like a lot of men involved at the time, may have gone under an assumed name, so he has found it difficult to cross-reference records. He remembers small details about him – white hair, the missing part of his finger and that he always sat in the kitchen of his small terraced house.

There was a range in one corner and his grandmother seemed always to be baking and cooking. Although a little detached from the family history, Peter speaks with fondness for his grandfather – so much so that I can't help but think the decision to sell the medals, this physical link to his past, and to the republic's troubled birth, is all the more baffling. Why not preserve them for the next generation? Ultimately, the decision to sell wasn't Peter's, but his father's.

'Essentially, my father would have them and they came out every year since they were awarded to my grandfather, sometime in the 1950s, I think. It was only when I was preparing them for sale I began to do a bit of research. My father is in and out of hospital – he's at that age. He said they could have been handed down to me, but he would prefer the money for them and to then give it out to the grandkids as a bonus for them.'

Along with the medals, Peter is also selling his grandfather's diary, in which he collected signatures during his internment. He has offered it online for €1,700, but says it could be worth more if the buyer can find de Valera's autograph in it.

Because he only saw them once in a while, Peter doesn't have the attachment to his grandfather's items that you might expect. There's also a more practical reason he says his father wants them to be sold. 'He doesn't want any friction or tension or legacy of that era to carry on for the next generation. Aside from what they mean symbolically, he didn't want to leave them to me and then for anyone else in the family to be bothered by that. So the cleanest thing to do was sell them and divide the money equally among the grandkids.'

The Weight of History

While the medals are over 50 years old, the diary is close to a century, and would be more important to the family. But in selling them both and breaking that link with the past, Peter and his family have been careful to ensure that whoever buys them will appreciate and have regard for them.

'To be honest, if they were mine I wouldn't be selling them,' Peter admits. 'But they are my dad's, and he has said to sell them and divide up the money. I think I would hold on to them.'

Peter heard talk that his grandfather did help break someone out of jail at one point, but he has spoken little to his own father about this whole aspect of the family history. That perhaps wouldn't be unusual for families who had grandparents involved in the Civil War or the War of Independence.

I recently spent time with relatives of the 'Men of the South' depicted in Seán Keating's painting. Many of their relatives fought in both the War of Independence and the Civil War, and what struck me was how little any of their sons, daughters, nieces and nephews had talked to their relatives about their time in the IRA. The Civil War in particular was almost too painful to acknowledge even for some of those who participated in it. And many grew bitter and disillusioned with the Ireland that emerged afterwards. And so it didn't strike me as all that unusual for Peter to have spoken very little to his father or grandfather

The Personals

about the background to the medals he was now entrusted with selling.

'Like a lot of families, it was sort of kept quiet,' Peter says. 'It wasn't really referred to – only maybe after my grandfather died. Maybe they talked more to the women in the family about it, but the men didn't really go into it. My father did say if I held on to the diary till 2021, around the time of the hundredth anniversary, I might get more for it. I was surprised how little interest there was in the medals in the end – maybe it's a sign the country is changing.'

Peter remains unapologetically Republican in his outlook, and believes that Brexit may provide an opportunity for a united Ireland in his lifetime. Although he acknowledges that for the younger generation it may not be as big a deal any more. 'They seem to be more interested in mobile phones and holidays than shooting each other over borders. In my grandfather's time, it was a lot bigger deal. I think we got complacent about the Irish Question since. Brexit might shake things up again. The main reason why we are selling these now, though, is because we want a clean break with history really. Hopefully someone else will appreciate them.'

Part Five
SENTIMENTAL VALUE

REKINDLING A ONE IN A MILLION CHANCE

Trying to contact X who taught maths in the 1970s. I tried to teach you to drive in my mini!!! He will be about 66 now. Would love to hear from you. *Online, January 2019*

'I really didn't expect anyone to contact me. In fact, I'd almost forgotten about that ad,' the 66-year-old retired teacher at the other end of the line tells me, after I reach out to her, having seen her ad in a lonely corner of the internet.

Once or twice before I've come across ads in which people are trying to find someone they knew in the past. In one case I remember, a son posted an ad in a local freesheet for several weeks looking for his father. There was no contact number or name provided with the ad, just a PO box. I wrote to it, asking if the person posting the ad would be interested in meeting me and

The Personals

explaining how I gathered the stories behind the ads. I never heard back.

Generally these ads are a shot in the dark after a lot of other avenues have been unsuccessfully explored. And to be fair, if I was going through the trauma of trying to make contact with someone I'd become distant from, for whatever reason, I'm not sure I'd want to share my story either.

What probably helps in this case is that the accent on the other end of the line is not Irish, and she later tells me she doesn't live in Ireland so does not mind going into some detail about why she posted the above ad. She tells me she grew up in the UK and went on to study art at university, and then had a four-decade art teaching career. At the time we talked she had only recently retired. She has no family links to Ireland that she knows of, and has lived a largely happy, fulfilled life.

A few months previously, she and a friend were thinking back to their college days. Maybe it was because she was retiring and moving into a new phase of life, but they spent an afternoon casting their minds back. They got talking about a former good friend. He was an Irishman who had worked in the same school as them and they'd all hung around as a group. Last time they'd all been together was in the late 1970s, and having tried all the usual social media routes to track him down, they decided to put some ads online in Ireland.

Rekindling a One in a Million Chance

'His surname is very common, like Smith or Jones, and he would be 66 years old now,' she tells me. 'We presume he went back to Ireland, possibly Dublin, in and around 1981 or 1982. To be honest, he was a bit of a ladies' man. He broke my heart. It was a strange relationship; a lot of them in the late seventies were! We were together a couple of years off and on, and we were good friends, but he liked to play the field. After a while, I met my husband and that was the end of it.'

She is a widow now, and over that coffee with her friend while they were reflecting on life on their own again, they'd thought about their former Irish friend and wondered what he could be up to. No one in their social circle has heard from him since he left. She knows he got engaged and that the engagement didn't last, and she thinks he may have got a promotion, but apart from that she has little information. She doesn't know anything about his family history or the area where he grew up, so has very few clues. Although she hasn't seen him in over four decades, she never really got over him.

'I really didn't,' she says. 'My husband and I had a different relationship. I met this man I would like to reconnect with when I was in my twenties and you get obsessive. I think when you are with someone you want them more really. I think I have matured now though about him. He was a very religious man, but something of a womaniser. I guess you can say sorry at the cathedral every Sunday, and off you go again. He was a very pretty boy, very attractive and a really nice guy.'

She is hoping that someone might see the ad, and given that it was free to post, she took a punt on it. It's been online so long though that she had genuinely forgotten she had posted it until I phoned her.

'I wasn't really expecting anything in terms of a response. It was a dare to put it online,' she explains. 'I tried all other ways of getting in touch so this was a last roll of the dice really. I was married when he left, and I did see him one last time at a party and that was about it really. He'd gone through another 20 women after he was with me before he disappeared.'

She says this man was typical of a lot of Irishmen at that time who came over to the UK, had several relationships, but ultimately were always going to return home. Their behaviour has to be seen in the context of the Ireland they were getting away from. It was a stifling society, where contraception was banned and the Church was still intent on meddling in what citizens did between the sheets.

'He was fanatical about his church,' she tells me. 'And of course, he was fond of the ladies. I knew he was playing the field and floating around, and we did become friends after we broke up.' Would she have married him? 'Yes, I think I would have, but I didn't think he would have married me, partly because I wasn't Catholic.'

Rekindling a One in a Million Chance

She thinks he could be in Canada or Australia and from time to time she imagines what he's doing. He always loved maths so he could be teaching that subject, or he could be working in banking, or he could still be connected to art in some way.

She taught art for 40 years and loved it to the end. Retirement was an adjustment, and was made all the more challenging by the fact that her husband had had a long illness and died not long before she stopped working. 'I'm enjoying my freedom now and my lovely pension,' she says. 'I'm conscious we're one of the last generation to get out with a decent pension. I am quite an anti-social person. I joined a few groups and widows' groups and they were very tame. They were full of nice sweet old ladies and it was a bit boring. I have my close friends and I see them and I have a few dogs. I haven't ruled out meeting someone else. I'm not that fond of being alone, to be honest. But as for online dating? Oh, God no! I put my name up ages ago on a dating site and within five minutes I got a lot of creepy replies and took my name off immediately. If I ever did it again I wouldn't put anything online any more in terms of dating, such as my name and age.'

I'm wondering what would happen if he turned up and was keen to meet her. Would it take much to rekindle their old romance? Would she forgive him? 'I'd have a decision to make, wouldn't I?' she says, laughing. 'It's a one in a million chance though. I doubt I will ever see him again.'

She says he may not even be alive, although he was always pretty fit so she has no reason to believe he isn't. He didn't drink or smoke and she would be curious to know what he looks like now, to see how kind the years may or may not have been. 'He actually looked like David Essex,' she says. 'He was a very pretty boy and had long mullet hair and I really was taken with him. That's about all I remember; a lot of it is forgotten in a haze. It was the 1970s after all!'

REMAINS OF A DETACHED DAY

Wanted: DVD of The Remains of the Day – the 1993 movie starring Anthony Hopkins.
Evening Echo

'How will I know which house is yours?' I ask the poster of the above advert, as he tried somewhat vaguely to give me directions. He's clearly surprised to have received a phone call within a few days of the ad appearing. But having trawled the ads for close to a decade, sometimes I just know when there's a story lying behind the few lines of text. Possibly it was the fact that *The Remains of the Day* wouldn't be everyone's cup of tea. It's a beautiful film, and one of my favourites, with the two main characters' unfulfilled love for each other mirroring the social repression of the time.

There's a sadness in the ad, as there has been with some other ads like this I've followed up. The placing

The Personals

of the ad is an admission in itself – that the person doesn't have a large circle of people to help locate the item, and perhaps doesn't have the resources or ability to order it online as many of us would. These are often the people on the fringes of technology, of society and ultimately of life.

'I'll place a used orange Calor gas cylinder outside the front wall of the house,' he tells me. An hour later, I find myself brushing past the cylinder and knocking on his front door. The front garden is unkempt and bare, and there are three painted concrete blocks on one side of the garden – perhaps a feature started a long time before but never fully realised.

The man meeting me has a baseball cap half on and half off his forehead as he guides me to a dusted-down chair in the middle of a cluttered sitting room. Every available seat is piled high with old newspapers and ring-stained coffee mugs. The walls are adorned with crumbling newspaper cuttings, mainly about George Best and Pelé, while dotted around the floor are two-litre Diet Coke bottles, some full, many half or fully empty. Needless to say, Francis Brennan would be horrified.

When the man speaks, he pauses for up to 30 seconds before saying something. Aside from the condition of their house, this is one of the first things I notice. It's almost as though he has to remember how to converse, what the protocol is and how to connect

Remains of a Detached Day

his thoughts with his words. I wonder when he last had a visitor. If he had not pulled a seat into the sitting room for me, there would have been nowhere to sit. It's not a room that is often shared.

He reaches for a pile of newspapers, pulls out a padded envelope and opens it. Inside is a well preserved second-hand copy of *The Remains of the Day*. It had arrived that morning. He already had it on VHS, and had worn it out because he watched it so often. The connection for him is with Anthony Hopkins and it was forged when he first saw the actor starring in *The Elephant Man* in a local cinema in 1980.

He tells me that he lives in this house with his brother, who is out, and that they grew up here and stayed on after their parents died. He doesn't have any friends. Aside from his brother, there is no one he is close to. He had spent three days on a training course decades earlier and that was the extent of his attempt to engage with getting a job. It wasn't for him. He has his obsessions: Hopkins, George Best, Pelé, New Order, Diet Coke.

He has never got beyond a cursory hello with a woman, and since his late teens he has constructed a world for himself which he has largely retreated into – a world he is both content with and trapped in.

We begin talking about the film. '*Remains of the Day* is one of my favourite films,' he tells me. 'Anthony Hopkins is my all-time favourite film actor and has

The Personals

been for a long number of years. My other favourite pastimes are music – listening to the popular music and the rock music. That film though I have watched many many times. Of the 35 films he was in from 1968 to 2005, made for cinema, I have learned the character names and lines of all of them. You see, Brian, I can have the way for retaining information all right.'

There are things he tells me he remembers that no one else does, such as dates. When he mentions a former priest in the area, he tells me not only how many years he lived locally, but the date he left, the dates he started his next post, how many years he has spent in his current parish and what date he started there. Dates are to his sanity what fixed rope points are to mountaineers. The other fixture in his life is his brother, with whom he has lived his entire life. Both of them were born in this house and continue to live in it beyond middle age.

'We get on very very well altogether, Brian. With our entire lives living here, we certainly didn't have any major bother between the two of us anyhow. There hasn't been a single bit of hassle in any way whatsoever.' He is lucid and speaks in a way that's genuine. He really only falters and stumbles when I ask whether he was ever tempted to marry.

'Well, ah.' Long pause. 'Sure, ah.' Another 30-second pause. He looks down at the stained carpet, then out the window and he's waiting for me to help him out with the question. I stay quiet. Eventually he says: 'I've never married, Brian, sure.'

'Did you come close to it?'

'Not really ... There's, ah ... Ah ... Well, how can I say it? For most of my life, Brian, there's never really been an interest. I can get along fine like. I get out to attend Mass, though I may not be perfectly pious. I know people to see them. I don't know people interpersonally. I don't have those kinds of relationships with people like that. I know them to say hello to them. But it stops there.'

He has never gone to a pub to have a drink with a friend in his life. He's been in them of course, but he never goes out of his way to go into them. "Tis only just the one day in the entire year that I take a drink and that's on Christmas Day. I take a drink of Guinness. Just the one 500ml can.'

As for some other people I've come across who live isolated lives, the act of putting an ad in the newspaper with a phone number attached is quite a public one, and somewhat at odds with their otherwise detached existence. At least that's what it looks like on the face of it. But as I spend more time with him, it becomes clear that the DVD request was his limited way of reaching out and feeling the embrace of society, albeit fleetingly. And it turns out that this isn't the first time he has used the small ads.

The Personals

'The last time I used the free ads was in 2014, and what was I looking for? Only the DVD of another film with Anthony Hopkins!' he says. 'It was a copy of *Amistad*, the film based around the lead up to the abolition of slavery. I got a reply and came across it on DVD so it was great. And then I did have an ad in the *Echo* free ads in 2005 as well. That was just looking for a video cassette copy of a music title by the rock group New Order. My three favourites in popular music were New Order, Rush and Bowie. I didn't get a single reply to that ad in 2005 though.'

Three times in the space of two decades he has reached out for some kind of human contact. Twice that has been successful, allowing him to continue with his preoccupations. He could have got the DVDs or the VHS tapes online, or asked his brother to pick them up on his way home. But that would have meant he was unlikely to have engaged with another human being during the process. It strikes me that while he was genuinely looking for a DVD when he placed his ad, he was also seeking to momentarily offset loneliness.

He leaves the house for Mass and the odd table quiz. That's it. Aside from some immediate family, he has no other connection with anyone outside these walls. He tells me that after I leave he will sit down and watch his new *Remains of the Day* DVD. He's comfortable answering my questions, although I sense there's a definite limit to how long he wants me to share his world. In total, I spend about 45 minutes with him before he decides it's time for me to go.

His face is beaming as we both inspect and approve the quality of the second-hand DVD that arrived in the post for him that morning courtesy of an *Echo* reader. Today's viewing will be the first of many he tells me proudly as I walk towards the door.

'It's a pity they never got together at the end,' he says, referring to the characters of Anthony Hopkins and Emma Thompson, who are clearly in love with each other but cannot express it. They're both trapped by convention, destined to live out occasionally contented but ultimately lonely and isolated lives, bound together in the shadows of fulfilment by their intimate detachment.

I reach out my hand to shake his and he thanks me for meeting him. As I walk away, I can hear him dragging the gas cylinder back to its position at the side of the house, where a large circular indentation in the grass, years in the making, was waiting for it.

GIVING A DOLL'S HOUSE A HOME

Gottschalk Antique Gabled Doll's House.
Rare 1920s doll's house in family for years.
All contents included. *DoneDeal, July 2018*

I'm in Meelick, a small village in east Clare, in a house off the Main Street, with two kittens on my lap and a cup of tea on the table. 'My name is Bernadette Ballarin,' my host tells me. 'My father is Italian and he's from Vittorio Veneto, in the north-eastern part of Italy. We lived in America and I was born and lived there until we moved here in 1977, because my mother is from the village. Basically, what happened was that my Irish granny got sick and my mother wanted to spend some time with her, because my mother had gone to America when she was 16 so she hadn't really seen her in years.'

Bernadette was 12 when her whole family moved to the small village in east Clare, and they lived in what was her grandmother's house. 'It was a huge culture shock,' she says. 'My parents bought this house which used to be an old shop and gutted it and refurbished it. I landed here from Connecticut, where we lived outside the town with very few neighbours, so on one level I was used to the quietness. I think probably the first thing to hit me was school, which was a really big culture shock. My saving grace was that I chose to go to school about 15 kilometres away in Shannon. This was the 1970s and I found a diverse student body there; a lot of Chileans fleeing the regime in their country had settled in Shannon and then you had people from Northern Ireland, so a huge influx of different cultures in the school, which suited me, but it was still a huge adjustment.'

For some, Shannon in the 1970s was a community for people from diverse backgrounds who, for whatever reason, had had to leave their own communities. While somewhat lacking in facilities and green spaces, it made up for that with an international outlook, and it was this exposure to other people and their beliefs that made school life at once fascinating and foreign for Bernadette, compared to high school in the US.

Among all the change and upheaval in her life, the one constant which accompanied Bernadette from the US back to Ireland was her beloved antique doll's house. Now what I know about antique doll's houses could be written on the back of a postage

The Personals

stamp, so not for the first time, I relied on my interviewee to take the lead, but not before I'd used my experience to mask my ignorance by teeing up the interviewee.

'So what's the story with this doll's house?'

'Well,' says Bernadette. 'The doll's house was in my grandmother's old house. She came from Italy and she moved to Connecticut. She was in a rented house first, and then they bought a big old farmhouse, and in the attic after they moved in they found this doll's house. I figure they would have moved in the early 1920s. This doll's house is a Gottschalk – he was a German doll's house manufacturer, and this is one of his original houses. He had many houses, but this one is one of the rarer ones.'

The house is so rare in fact that Bernadette thinks there are maybe only two or three left in existence that are exactly like this one. I wouldn't be admitting this to the lads in the golf club, but it really is a beautiful piece of art. Gottschalk created a series of townhouses as well as country houses and because people threw them out over the years, Bernadette believes there are not many left in their original state. There was a time in the 1970s and 1980s when they weren't in vogue.

It's the kind of item you could imagine *Antiques Roadshow* assessors getting teary-eyed over, which end up on YouTube clips. They'd prod and poke with gloved hands and give a high valuation, to many oohs

Giving a Doll's House a Home

and aahs, with the owners saying they would never sell, although in their minds they are already walking on that beach outside an exclusive resort in Bali.

Bernadette's grandmother found this house and kept it from the 1920s onwards. The previous owners had also been immigrants to the US. She knows that because her granny often said that the people she bought the house from couldn't speak a whole lot of English. The doll's house was left in the attic most of the time, until it was passed down to Bernadette as the youngest grandchild, and it has remained with her since.

For something that has criss-crossed continents, it is remarkably well-preserved; everything from the miniature stairs to the small curtains hanging in the windows are original, and date back possibly to the end of the nineteenth century or the beginning of the twentieth at the latest. For years, Bernadette had kept it in her bedroom. It gave her a sense of home after she left the US, and it took her back not only to Connecticut, but also to her grandmother and those family ties she had left behind.

'It contains lovely fond memories for me, but I don't have any kids, so what do I do with it?' she says, holding the house up for me to see the craftsmanship underneath. 'I just think if I die tomorrow there will be a skip outside that door within five minutes and someone will either sell it or dump it, so this way I get to pick and choose how I want to leave it and where I want it to go. It's time it got a new home and another generation can enjoy it.'

To give the doll's house another lease of life will cost any prospective buyer just shy of €2,000. That's a lot of wedge for something which has heritage and is an antique and a slice of history, but if bought for a child is still essentially a toy. So, who exactly is going to buy it? 'I've had two calls from a museum in Switzerland that want to take it,' she tells me. 'I'm kind of thinking though: do I really want it to be in a museum? I think I would prefer it to go to a family as opposed to a museum. I also had a phone call from two boys who were going to a college in Tralee and doing some kind of film-making project. They wanted the house to blow it up! Their plan was to take it and put it in a field and they were going to do something weird and wonderful with it. But they really just wanted to blow it up, because it was exactly like this house somewhere down in Cork they spotted.'

Having kept the doll's house all these years, surely she was hardly likely to consider handing it over to two students from Tralee to blow it up in a field? 'Yah, I know!' she says, laughing. 'I said, "Lads, I'm really sorry, much and all as I would love to help you with

Giving a Doll's House a Home

your project, but I am not giving you the house to blow up." They said, well look, we can pool together a load of us and we think we can come up with about €400. I said, "Lads, it's not happening ..."'

Apart from the museum and the students, no one else has phoned about the doll's house, so Bernadette says she will keep the ad up and hold out until the right buyer comes along. As we both imagine who that might be – a family perhaps, or maybe someone trying to reconnect with their own childhood, Bernadette tells me more about her family circumstances. Life hasn't been easy for her in recent years. She was living in Ennis in her own home, but events meant she had to return to her childhood home at very short notice.

'My mother had an aneurysm in her tummy and went in for a routine enough operation and didn't come home,' she says. 'It was a genetic issue – her brothers and sister had the same, and they all came out of it fine but she didn't. Then the day of her funeral, Dad got a stroke. I didn't have a chance to grieve; my mum had been caring for my dad, as he had had a stroke a few years earlier. And then, boom, this happens; suddenly I had to cut my hours at work, move back in here and plan my life around him. But I did it because that's just what you do.'

Bernadette has come through that interesting point on the circle of life. When we are infants our parents care for us and ensure we make it to the next stage,

The Personals

and sometimes at the end of their lives we get to return that favour. 'I wouldn't have it any other way,' she says.

I ask Bernadette if she had had children of her own, would she have kept the house? 'Absolutely, I would,' she says. 'I was married. Not any more. It's a good thing I'm not married any more as I'm too odd! I didn't have kids and now I have this beautiful doll's house and no one to give it to.'

She'll be sad to be parted from it, but with both her parents now dead, she's surrounded by enough memories having moved back into her family home, and maybe doesn't want to be burdened with any more.

'You know what, it's life,' she says. 'I've let go of lots of things. I've come to a time in my life where I can say this was a beautiful piece of furniture in my life and now I have the memories and it's great, but I really need to let it go ...'

Part Six
COLLECTORS

'WE ARE COLLECTORS ... AND WE WILL DIE AS COLLECTORS'

Wanted: any GAA-related material pre-1975. Very good prices paid for good collections of same. *Evening Echo, August 2018*

I'm fairly confident in saying this is one of the longest-running classified ads in the *Evening Echo*. It runs every week and has done for the last 15 years or so. The person behind this ad also publishes several others on a weekly basis. One is more specific and is looking for 1930s and 1940s Munster hurling and football final programmes, while another is looking for old Wavin hurleys, the type used in primary schools to stop fellas getting lumps knocked out of them in the name of sport. He's what I would call a semi-professional collector, and one of dozens who pop up from time to time in the small ads.

Throughout the classified ads, from eBay to DoneDeal, the *Farmers Journal* to the *Evening Echo*,

The Personals

you'll find private collectors. Generally, these are people who have become fixated on their subject matter and are hoping to chance upon items people may have in their attic without realising their value. Alternatively, collectors will use the ads to sell and trade their excess stock.

Few of them I've met down through the years are as obsessive and committed as the man behind this ad. For security reasons he prefers not to be named or have his location disclosed. He describes himself as one of the top 15 private collectors of GAA memorabilia in the country.

I met him at his home in the west of Ireland where in the middle of the kitchen table were piles of folders, boxes full of medals and some very old hurleys. Some of the programmes are just one page, tattered and frayed at the edges, and covered with plastic sleeves so they can be carefully filed away. He works a regular job, has a college-going family and is a big GAA fan. I get the sense that he's thrilled to have someone to discuss the collection with.

I'm keen to know how someone goes from attending games to obsessively collecting related memorabilia. What are the impulses that lead someone to putting an advertisement in a newspaper regularly for 15 years in the hope of finding a 70-year-old programme from a long-forgotten Munster final?

'We Are Collectors ... and We Will Die as Collectors'

'I started going to matches in 1980,' he tells me. 'I was 11 or 12 years of age. I also had a natural collector's instinct. I collected stamps from the age of five and collected coins from the age of six and then I started collecting newspapers at the age of eight – the *Irish Independent* mainly. A lot of collectors like paper. I know one, for example – a GAA person – who has been cutting out newspapers since 1949. It's a total collector mentality. I firmly believe that it is a form of obsessive compulsive disorder. I know a lot of collectors, mostly GAA people, and we're all on some kind of spectrum, I think. I collect very specific high-quality items which sometimes cost me a lot of money. I am doing this to have the definitive collection of, in this case, Limerick GAA-related material.'

I find the idea that collecting is some form of early therapeutic intervention fascinating. As I spend time with him, the intensity of his passion for collecting becomes clear. It's juxtaposed with his regular life, and maybe collecting keeps a part of his mind occupied that might otherwise find a more destructive or unhealthy outlet. The deal he has struck with his wife is that items can only be kept downstairs for a few weeks, then they need to be stored somewhere out of the way. He's a very private man and putting advertisements in the classified section of the *Evening Echo* every week as he has done for the past 15 years seems at odds with his desire for confidentiality.

The Personals

'The advantage of the *Evening Echo* to me is that it hits Cork city. It's also free and I can put in that ad every single week and hit my demographic, which is a sports-mad GAA-supporting audience in Cork. And aside from publishing my number it's relatively anonymous.'

In the decade and a half he's been putting the ad in the paper, he reckons he's met people and bought their full collections at least a dozen times. In one case he met an older woman whose husband had recently died. This man had gone to all the Cork GAA matches, both hurling and football, and his box of programmes was stuck in a corner of a room. 'She pulled it out a year or two after he died and was wondering what to do with it,' he tells me. 'Then she sees my ad, gives me a call and I go see her and pay, I think, about €600 for the full collection. I took it away, broke it up and kept what I wanted and then tried to either swap the rest or sell it.'

He takes pride in telling me he is now one of the largest private collectors in the country. When he began going to games in 1980 he collected all the programmes, and so had a full set of programmes from games he attended until 1997. This was the kick-start for his collection. Of course, like any good collector he couldn't stop at that. At a small collectible shop in Dublin in the summer of 1997, he saw the 1963 and 1965 All-Ireland final programmes for sale, which happened to have a

'We Are Collectors ... and We Will Die as Collectors'

Limerick minor team playing. 'I said to myself: I have all the programmes from 1980 and Limerick don't get to too many All-Irelands, so I bought the two All-Ireland programmes for a total of £36.'

And of course, once he had the All-Ireland final programmes he needed to go back and look for the Munster final programmes for both years. You can see where this is going, can't you?

Will he ever be able to say his collection is complete? 'It's never really complete. I am back to 1944 in Limerick senior hurling championship programmes, but I am missing a lot of programmes from the 1930s,' he says. 'Limerick played in five All-Ireland finals in the 1930s. In the 21 years I have been collecting I have only ever been able to purchase one of them. It was in an auction down in Kilkenny. A lot of collectors like myself have very few All-Ireland programmes from before the war. The programmes of the 1930s and 1940s tended just to be one sheet. In those times, very few people kept anything. We have about 12 to 15 big collectors in the country. I am one of them but the other collectors tend to collect all competitions and I only collect Limerick so I'm not seen as a risk to any of these other guys.'

Browsing through his collection of 1,000 or so programmes, I find that it ranges from All-Ireland finals to League finals, Railway Cups to regional championships as well as county, club, minor, under-

21 and senior games. I wonder what has been his best find through the *Evening Echo* ads?

'The best find I had was the proceeds of an old collector about six or seven years ago outside Cork. His nephew called me and said he collected a lot. That can mean anything of course, but really the litmus test is anyone who has programmes before 1975, because that's when programmes start having a value really. This man had a few thousand programmes, and some excellent GAA newspapers from the 1950s and 1960s. He had protected the stuff really really well. He actually had a little tomb, like a back room, which when you opened it up was like Tutankhamun's vault. On all sides were shelves and I bought the whole collection. It took me three trips up and down to Cork before I had it all taken away.'

I can't help but think of my interviewee's family, as he arrives home from Cork with the car stuffed with GAA annuals, programmes and old newspapers. Does his wife share his glee when he arrives in the front door with another box full of dusty programmes? 'She is absolutely appalled,' he tells me. 'She really detests it. We have two kids who have asthma, so it's not good. I'm allowed to decontaminate them in that room out there and then I have to move them within two months. So either upstairs, out in the shed or moved on.'

Does he regard collecting as an addiction? 'It's an obsession,' he says. 'Plus, I love meeting people. I

'We Are Collectors ... and We Will Die as Collectors'

have met some of the best people through collecting. And when we go up to the All-Ireland finals we will meet up. I consider myself a GAA man first, and a collector second.'

The most he had spent on one programme was €1,400 for the 1933 All-Ireland final programme. He says it shouldn't have cost him that much, but another collector bid against him. Often they do side deals between themselves to prevent that happening, but that didn't work on this occasion. He rarely gets hits online, but has noticed in the past year or so that he's getting fewer calls through the newspaper classifieds.

Having built up this amazing collection over the years, I'm curious to know how often he takes it out and looks at it. 'Very rarely,' he says. 'I've no interest in looking at it. The joy is in having it and knowing that if someone comes to me looking for a programme from, say, 1947, I can pull it out and say, yep, I have that programme. So I tend not to look at the collection at all, I only ever focus on what I am missing. The joy for me is having rare items no one else will have. For example, *Gaelic Sport* was a very seminal old GAA magazine that ran from 1958 right through to 2002 and I know that there were 417 editions of it. I have two full runs of it, which is five boxes of it, in the house here. I built one run and then a collector gave me a second run which was in better condition and I couldn't part with either of them.'

The Personals

It's this kind of attention to detail that separates the casual collector from the serious one. Long after I turn off the tape recorder we're still sitting at his kitchen table leafing through his collection. His passion is infectious, as is his general sports knowledge, and I jokingly say he'd be some man to have on a table quiz team. I wonder was it in some way a therapy for him over the years to channel his compulsions into collecting?

'I don't really see it as that. I see myself as a very focused collector. I would look on it as being a collector gene,' he says, 'rather than something that was a mutation or sickness. We are collectors. We were collectors from a young age, and we will die as collectors.'

SIGNING THE PAST AWAY

Nelson Mandela hand-signed autograph.
Genuine hand-signed piece, doing a clear-out, reason for quick sale, €3,000.
DoneDeal, October 2018

Under his bed in his parents' house in rural Cork, John has a box that once contained items that meant the world to him. Now in his early thirties, he's leaving Cork and making the move to Dublin. The psychological break with his home county has meant that it's finally time to get rid of his treasured autograph collection. The itch has been scratched. He's not in his twenties any more and the obsession has abated. Plus, the few bob he expects to get will come in handy when he finds himself shelling out up to €2,000 a month for a glorified cupboard in Dublin 15.

For now though, John wants to take me back to when he first began an autograph collection, and much

The Personals

to my surprise, he credits one Charles J. Haughey with kick-starting his passion. 'Ex-Taoiseach Charles Haughey and I wrote to each other a lot when I was in Leaving Cert,' John tells me. 'I was doing honours history and we had to do a project on a subject or a person in time. So I decided to write to Charlie Haughey. This was back in 1997 and he was a former Taoiseach at the time.'

Don't you just love Ireland? That adage that you're only ever two phone calls away from a minister, or a Taoiseach in this case, is true. John had developed an interest in current affairs, and he wanted to have a discussion with the former Taoiseach and get his views on the events of the day. He also had one eye on the 30 per cent of the marks given for his final-year history project, and he probably figured that not too many in his class would have a former head of state contributing. 'I was just chancing my arm writing to him really,' says John. 'But in fairness to him, he wrote back swiftly and said he was very happy to oblige. Over the course of a year we wrote back and forth. He would write on headed notepaper and gave me his views on lots of things, including a documentary that was broadcast on RTÉ at the time about him and other things of interest.'

At one stage Haughey sent a signed portrait of himself to John, and at various other times over the years he sent cards with pictures of Kinsealy and of course, his autograph. Unsurprisingly, John got full marks for the project and an 'A' in the Leaving Cert exam. The experience accelerated his interest in historical figures and events and his autograph collecting obsession began in earnest, thanks to Charlie.

Sometimes what draws me into an ad like this is not so much the item for sale, but the words used to sell it. In this case, of course the Mandela name is interesting, but possibly more interesting was the fact that the seller was doing a clear-out and that there was a reason for a quick sale.

Quick sale often means either a fresh start or an attempt to break free from past associations or debt. It can signify a break-up, a rebirth, economic difficulty or someone wanting to move on from grief or loss. In this case, as I was to find out, it meant a new beginning, a move away from home and the start of a new life.

Over the years John would go to fairs and auctions and keep an eye out online for any interesting autographs that came up. He bought a copy of Margaret Thatcher's biography signed by her before she became ill. Like many of the collectors gathered together in this book, he became obsessive about his pursuit, and began taking courses in how to identify fake or real autographs. Generally, autographs are collected by enthusiasts who attend book signings by famous people, or go to personal appearances. At these you pay a fee for the privilege of having their scribble.

The Personals

There are several companies that will authenticate autographs and sometimes even provide a photo of the person signing the autograph as further proof.

Through this process John acquired the Nelson Mandela autograph which he has now put up for sale. It had been in a book originally and he has the photo of Mandela signing to prove its authenticity. He later acquired Richard Nixon's signature by buying it directly from a person who lived next door to Nixon in California, and with that autograph he also got a picture of the seller with Nixon.

In total, he's had seven US presidents' autographs which he can authenticate. This is important, he says, because a lot of these being sold online are made with an auto pen machine. The number of these kinds of automated autographs doing the rounds prompted John to take an online course in autographs just so he could tell the difference between those written by hand and those written by machine.

Following on from this, he became fascinated with the way autographs had been written, and he became interested in the kind of pens people used to sign their names. This led him to buying the pen Lyndon B. Johnson used to sign several deals. The other presidential autographs he has include those of Jimmy Carter, the two Bushes and Bill Clinton, as well as many Irish political leaders, from Jack Lynch to Garret FitzGerald.

Signing the Past Away

Now John has taken a job in Dublin, he's clearing out his old room, and selling what he doesn't want any more. He was previously offered a lot of money for some of the collection, including the Mandela autograph. This was at a time when many of the figures, such as Thatcher, were alive. He expects his collection may make more now that several have passed away. He needs to make as much as he can, given the way rents in Dublin are escalating. He talks about this several times during the course of our interview. It says something when a mid-career civil servant can't readily afford to rent in Dublin. We talk about the possibility that people like him will increasingly remain in Cork in years to come and commute daily to Dublin instead of paying upwards of €500 a week for a room. He reminds me that rents in Cork are not far behind those in Dublin.

The high rents mean getting rid of a collection which is personal to him, but which he rarely shares with others, so it's a sacrifice he is willing to make. Anyway, the thrill in building the collection wasn't in having a huge archive of material in his room. It was in combining his interest in history with something personal to a figure of great historical interest, something that came from their very fingertips – that was the buzz for him.

Not unusually for a collector, his was a relatively narrow focus. Present-day Hollywood stars don't

The Personals

interest him. He's had the autographs of Bob Hope, Jimmy Stewart and a few others during his time collecting and is more interested in old-school film idols. In other words, don't expect him to be pursuing the scribblings of the Kardashians online any time soon.

When he had his full collection, he had the autographs mounted and displayed in his bedroom, and later, when he had a home office, they were hung there. The most he'd paid for an autograph was for Nelson Mandela's, which was around €1,000. He was offered €2,500 for it, but decided instead to put it under his bed for a few years in the hope of achieving a higher price when the great man passed on. So far, that hasn't quite worked out, and the move to Dublin fund is looking a lot leaner because of it.

The one autograph he wanted and could never get his hands on was that of US President John F. Kennedy. 'I had a few bids all right for one but never got near it,' he said. 'I would have had Ted Kennedy. I had JFK's Mass card and stuff but never got JFK's signature. I would have needed about $10,000 for it and that's way out of my league,' he tells me. 'If I ever have the money though I will buy it. I would love to have it. He was a big hero of mine. Because he died young, some people think there's not many of his autographs out there. He signed a lot of letters as a senator though and a lot of those letters are out there somewhere.'

Signing the Past Away

Moving on to Irish historical autographs, he's always had his eye on the big two of Collins and de Valera. He tells me that a German autograph house has bought a lot of Irish autographs in recent years, including those of Douglas Hyde and others and many are now in private collections. 'You can expect to pay up to €5,000 for de Valera's autograph,' he says, adding that he knows people who have one through their parents but would never sell.

We discuss how much Charlie Haughey's autograph is likely to be worth in the decades ahead and I mention that the only time I saw Haughey publicly was at former Taoiseach Jack Lynch's funeral in Cork. I was standing on Patrick Street with thousands of others, and Haughey was in a car in the funeral procession, and the abuse hurled at him was quite something.

'I was so embarrassed and sorry that happened,' John says. 'There is no place for that. I was there and I introduced myself to him after and he said it's so nice to meet and thanks for saying hello. I was so embarrassed. It was not the time and place for it. We are better than that. Cork people are better than that. I was told shortly after the funeral he told the driver just to go straight home. It is a pity.'

That reaction has to be seen in the context of Haughey and Lynch's complex relationship, as well as the fall from grace and controversy surrounding the former Taoiseach. He was obviously one of the most capable politicians we've ever produced on this island, and also one of the most flawed.

'My parents are in their seventies and they will tell you he was a good Taoiseach,' John says. 'He did a lot of good things, such as what he did for the arts and the elderly and a lot of it gets overshadowed. You take my mother's generation, for example, very few will have a bad word to say about him. OK, there's his personal life and everything, but sure everyone has something. He was a divisive figure, but as far as I'm concerned, in terms of my interactions with him, he couldn't have been more helpful. He wrote to me about a dozen times and he really didn't have to; there was nothing in it for him.'

During that correspondence, they discussed a recent programme made about the ex-Taoiseach on television which had been complimentary about him, and Haughey also discussed going into coalition with the PDs, as well as ranking formidable political opponents. John looks back on the exchanges with Haughey as having had a big influence on his passions and interests in life that have sustained him to this day. He doubts, though, that the Haughey autograph will hold its value.

Having said that, sometimes you can't tell which autographs will end up increasing in value. For example, he has had the Mandela autograph for sale a while and is surprised there hasn't been more interest. It's likely to be sold to someone in business who wants to put it on the wall of their office. 'Maybe the price is putting people off, but to be totally honest, there was more interest in his autograph when he was alive than now when he is dead,' he tells me.

He reflects back on some of the other valuable autographs he's owned over the years, such as Jimmy Stewart's. Darwin's is one he would like to get his hands on, and he says it's always worth looking inside old books in charity shops for signatures. He advises caution when buying autographs online though as there are a lot of forgeries around. The best way to authenticate an autograph is to get it direct from the person themselves at a book signing, or to write to them as he did. Haughey wasn't the only head of state he wrote to. When he was in office, he chanced his arm and wrote to Prime Minister Tony Blair. 'I just thought I'd try it and ask him for his autograph,' John says. 'I used a bit of the Irish *plámás* about how I was building up a collection and told him he would be a fantastic addition. He had no problem writing back on official paper with his autograph enclosed. It sometimes pays to have a bit of neck!'

John has also had a few Reagan autographs over the years, and would love to get his hands on Churchill's. His is hard to get though, unlike Thatcher's, which is fairly ubiquitous in the autograph world.

The Personals

Much of the collection is gone now and he's left with about 20 autographs. Haughey, Nelson Mandela and Bill Clinton are the stand-out ones. The collecting bug which sustained him for so many years has left him. Life has taken over. In a way, I tell him, he's one of the lucky ones, in that some collectors find it very difficult to ever manage an amicable divorce from their passion, and it ends up becoming a burden.

For John, the rents in Dublin mean that the only signature he's likely to be seeing for a while is his own at the bottom of inflated lease agreements. Despite that, he's relishing the move.

Part Seven
LOST CAUSES?

BEING FRANK

Help wanted for pensioner to formulate a difficult letter. *Evening Echo*

The last page of the classifieds is often where the nuggets are, where requests that don't fit into other categories find a home. You can find everything from people hoping to meet long-lost friends to a whole series of anonymous devotions to Catholic saints, the offer of miracle cures or the contact details for addiction counselling services. Some time ago, my eye was drawn to the above advertisement.

From experience, anyone who feels they need to post an ad like this in the small ads possibly lives something of an isolated life, whether by design or accident. It also struck me as unusual that the number provided was a landline number in an era when mobile phones are ubiquitous. I was curious to find out why the letter the person needed help with was so difficult

The Personals

– was it a legal issue perhaps? Or something emotional that had to be penned to a long-lost relative? Or the ending of an affair maybe? As you can probably tell, I wasn't doing a great job in reining in my imagination in advance of making contact.

When I did eventually phone the number provided, an elderly man with a slightly unusual accent answered. He told me he had put the advertisement in the *Evening Echo* for several weeks running. As we got chatting, Frank told me he was applying for a pension, having worked with an 'agency' in Europe for a long period of time. He referenced the fact that his work was 'top secret', and had implications for the whole of the human race.

As you may have gathered from previous stories, you sometimes find interesting characters like Frank through the classified ads – people who perhaps (and I hope I'm not being unkind when I say this) don't fit in easily elsewhere. It makes complete sense to me that they fit perfectly on the pages of the personals and the small ads. There's a kinship of sorts between the lonely and the lost, the eccentric and the strait-laced in the personals.

I meet Frank at his home. The house appeared to be under renovation, with a large tarpaulin and building blocks in the front garden and the contents inside piled high, with dust covering many surfaces. Frank had untidy hair and oversized Guinness slippers on his feet. He apologised for the condition of the house, and made a reference to building work taking place, but as he dusted down a surface for me to sit on, it became clear that there was no construction work on-going. This was how he lived – on an imitation building site, with layers of dust and rubble and crates for seats. There were small stacks of used beer mats, unfinished antique restoration furniture, and piles and piles of frayed documents and scraps of paper.

Little light shone through the windows as the overgrown garden obscured them, creating a sort of evening dimness all day long inside the house. He spoke in half-finished sentences and was both vague and certain, distant and very present. There was nothing to sit down on in any of the rooms besides the one stool he sat on – no chair without mounds of items piled high on it, which told me that he rarely if ever had visitors.

A few weeks before I met Frank, I had watched the film *A Beautiful Mind*, in which Russell Crowe plays the brilliant academic John Nash who had won a Nobel Prize. In one scene in the film, the character's cluttered mind is outwardly manifested in the delusions he has when he fills the garden shed with scraps of paper and clutter. That scene came back to me as I stood against a large pile of dusty records and looked around Frank's sitting room. Perhaps this is what isolation, loneliness and mental illness looks like.

The Personals

His environment was evidence that the balance between reality and fiction had not just tilted, but toppled. I couldn't help wondering when the last time footsteps other than Frank's had been heard on the creaky stained floorboards in his hall. So as not to make him feel uncomfortable, I decide to keep up the pretence that Frank really is waiting on builders and that all this dusty chaos is just a temporary inconvenience, as opposed to day-to-day life. 'A good builder is harder to find than an All-Ireland medal in Mayo,' I say, trying to lighten the mood.

Frank wants to get down to business and go into why I'm here, so I ask him why he took out the advertisement. 'I have had little success in connecting with the [European] authorities, partly through the language barrier and because they don't seem to have a very good communication system,' he explains. 'I worked there for years and my pension has been held up in red tape. It's been going on for almost a year.'

I've decided by this point that there is unlikely to be an authority which has withheld Frank's pension. I'm not even sure if he's ever been to the country he keeps referencing. He repeats what he told me on the phone, that he worked for an agency, and that much of the work was confidential. I say that it's not like private companies to try to get out of paying for pensions, and we laugh, but all the while he's checking me out, wondering perhaps how much of his story I believe.

Being Frank

One woman has responded to his advertisement and as she is a native speaker, she has offered to communicate to the particular authorities on his behalf. 'I perceive myself now as being just a number,' Frank tells me. The more we go into his story, the more we get to the essence of Frank and the more I come to like him. I've always been drawn to people on the fringes and, to be honest, I have no idea why. The drifters, the dropouts, the difficult personalities and the loners fascinate me and draw me in far more than the popular level-headed types you meet more regularly.

Frank and I spoke for a while longer. Maybe he did have a pension issue, and maybe the builders were going to return to his house some day. But the likelihood is that Frank had slipped through the cracks, and was desperately trying to hold on to the foundations above his head where his sanity once lay.

I passed an hour in his company and after the initial few minutes chat about the ad and the need for a letter writer, we didn't mention it again. He skipped from topic to topic. I'm guessing that putting an ad in the paper was possibly a way of staving off loneliness, of having some kind of human contact or breaking through the silence and the solitude.

We spoke about politics and religion, about the EU and the UK, about leaves in autumn and where birds go in spring. We talked about Dublin and Paris, about west Cork and Budapest – it was akin to speaking to

The Personals

the physical embodiment of a BBC Radio 4 magazine programme, just a little more detached. And then, almost without warning, Frank began walking to the front door.

He had had enough human contact maybe, or he had shared his cluttered space for as long as he wanted to. I mumbled something about hoping he would keep me updated about whether or not the pension was sorted, and it almost seemed to be news to him that there was a pension to be sorted.

'Yes, sure,' he said, as we shook hands and he looked out of the door beyond me to see if anyone else had noticed he'd had a visitor – an actual human interaction. I walked away thinking that Frank didn't need someone to write a letter for him, he just needed someone to talk to, someone to be human with.

BUILDING A BIGGER SHRINE

> **Lost 20 July Blackpool Post Office, sum of money, my pension.** If anyone hands it over, I would be grateful. *Evening Echo, September 2018*

Less than a year after his death in 1232, Anthony of Padua, the son of a wealthy and noble Portuguese family, was canonised by Pope Gregory IX and became better known as St Anthony. Wikipedia tells us he is especially 'invoked and venerated all over the world as the patron saint for the recovery of lost items and is credited with many miracles involving lost people, lost things and even lost spiritual goods'. So for almost 800 years, people have been pleading with Anthony of Padua to recover lost things: wallets, keys, minds, marriages; you name it, Anthony is the go-to saint for the hopeless. One would think then that someone with a particularly strong devotion to St Anthony should

The Personals

have no need to be placing ads in newspapers when they misplace something …

Which brings us neatly to the north side of Cork city and Paul, a sixty-something retired grandfather, who has not one but two shrines to St Anthony in his home. Every week Paul collects his pension in the same post office in Blackpool in Cork. And every week he divides it the same way – €170 into one pocket for his wife and the bills, and €70 into his other pocket, which is his own spending money for the week. 'I went to collect the pension and met a friend at the Post Office,' he tells me. 'We went up the escalator and then walked down the steps beside it. I put my hand in my pocket. No €170. Not there. Checked. Gone. It was sickening and very upsetting. I was gutted actually but my wife just said OK, get over it, and we moved on.'

In the days immediately after it happened, while Paul was trying to get over his loss, he decided to put an ad in the paper, saying that he'd lost a sum of money, and to run it over a few weeks. In the two weeks before I met him, he had updated the ad to add the fact that it was his pension. His hope is that someone may have picked up the money, would see his ad, feel guilty and return it. Eh right, good luck with that, I tell him.

While he was fairly annoyed that two-thirds of his weekly income had been lost in one go, unfortunately,

Building a Bigger Shrine

it's not the first time Paul has lost money. 'I'm very careless,' he admits. 'I have to get a tracksuit with a zip in the pocket. I *have to*. The thing about it is I was very, very disappointed and I had lost smaller amounts before out of my pocket. Why me? When you're working, you can take on a bit of overtime or whatever and try and make it up. But you can never make up a pension.'

Has he had many responses to the ad that has been running for a few weeks? 'None,' he says. 'And to be honest, I can't imagine anyone giving me a ring. It was last chance saloon putting that ad in.'

Speaking of last chances, I ask Paul if he is a religious man, a weekly Mass-goer perhaps? 'No Mass,' he says, 'but I pray every day. I've a shrine up in the kitchen. Every day I pray to St Anthony.'

'Hang on! St Anthony? The lost causes guy?' I say. 'So, is he on a couple of weeks' holiday or what?'

'He must have gone away on holidays all right!' says Paul, laughing, 'But he's back again. My wife and I are St Anthony people. My wife is a churchgoer all the time but what the priest says I don't believe in it. I have my own religion here and I have a shrine up beside me in the bed also.'

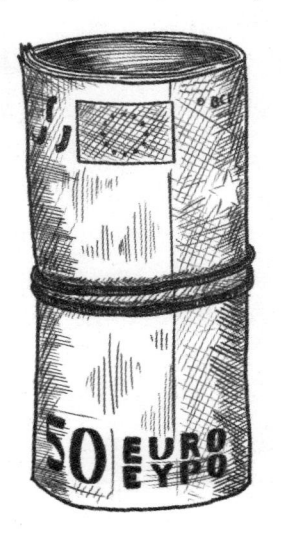

203

The Personals

Paul and his wife had met almost 50 years earlier in a ballroom in Blarney. They then lost touch for two years, and reconnected and married shortly after. They have been married for 46 years and have four children and four grandchildren, with another on the way. So, with half a century of marriage behind them, I'm curious to know the secret to a long marriage.

'There has to be a lot of love involved,' he says sincerely. 'I'm 72 and I am mad about her. I love her. She is everything to me. She's not a pub person but is very active with various groups and whatnot. I can live on a pension. Since I retired, I never asked her for a penny for drink and I don't drink weekdays – just maybe on a Sunday I'll go for a few drinks.'

The love he and his wife have sustained for nearly half a century is refreshing, and so too is the ease with which he is able to discuss his feelings for her with me. I am a total stranger he has met only an hour or so earlier, and yet here he is talking candidly about the intensity of his devotion to her. Marriage is often represented in cynical and jaded terms in popular culture, and we're told that Irish men struggle with their emotions, particularly those of an older generation. Paul didn't fit that narrative and also didn't fit the stereotype of the Irish male and their discomfort at opening up about their emotions. Perhaps you reach a stage in your life when you don't feel the need to reaffirm your maleness in the way society prescribes any more, and you realise what's really important and how lucky you are to have such intense love. Or, as Paul succinctly puts it: 'People think you can't be upfront about how you feel for someone and be macho at the same time. I think that's a load of codswallop.'

It's time for me to leave and Paul wants me to know it is the first time he has used the small ads. If someone happens to respond with the money, he says he will provide a reward. He tells me he's a man who likes routine, so the loss of money really impacted on him. With that in mind, I'm wondering did he go for a few drinks the week he lost the money as he usually does? 'No,' he says laughing. 'I was afraid. It came to the Sunday and she said to me, "I want you to go up there." I am blessed with her and I can always turn to that. Even though this was a big loss for me, look what I have. I have so much more than wealth. As for the pension? I will have to get a wallet, or a zipped pocket or maybe a bra to put it in ...'

Or maybe, I tentatively suggest, a bigger shrine to St Anthony?

Part Eight
THIS MORTAL COIL

MEETING A MAN ABOUT A HEARSE

Horse-drawn Victorian hearse, very old. For restoration. Circa 1870. Original condition, needs slight work to restore. Might consider part exchange. Also selection of traps and carriages. €2,850. ***DoneDeal, July 2017***

What drew me to this ad were key words I've come to spot over the years that signal there's likely to be a story behind the text. Generally, when words such as 'restoration' or key dates, such as the 1870s in this case, are given then you can be fairly sure this isn't a chance find someone is trying to offload. Reading the ad, the idea that a private individual in a rural location would have a nineteenth-century horse-drawn hearse in the shed, but also the fact that he might consider a part exchange is intriguing. I mean, who wants to swap something for a Victorian hearse? I'm

The Personals

trying to envisage the scenario: 'Tell you what, I'll give you €500 cash and I'll throw in the Punto ...'

Clearly, I had to meet the man behind it, and so one grey afternoon I found myself in a village called Boherbue on the Cork/Kerry border where Mike Fleming lives. I was at his home near a crossroads, and it soon became clear I was meeting someone who shared my fascination (bordering on obsession) with classified ads.

Mike has a thriving commercial business, as well as some land and property, and he is the kind of man who has a wide range of interests and has built several varied collections over his lifetime. He also struck me as the type of person who, while maintaining an overall passion for historical items, could lose interest in an item quickly, and needs to move on to the next thing. The thrill of the hunt is in the chase ...

Dotted around his property were many items of historical interest, from old labouring tools to a collection of vintage tractors and ploughs, to old bar signs, vintage cars and old bottles. There was even a museum scene depicting an Irish Famine wake in one corner of an outhouse, complete with life-size figures and a realistic-looking dead body in a bed. I mean, go figure.

After work in the evenings, when some people are sitting down to a night of Netflix or *The Late Late Show*, Mike Fleming opens his laptop and scours the small ads. The inside of his sheds looks like a holding warehouse for DoneDeal, such is the variety and volume of items. As we stroll round, his depth of knowledge is impressive, but so too is the responsibility he feels as the keeper of traditions and customs and ways. As the poet once said, if we only had old Ireland back again …

His collecting began, as with many collectors in this book, in childhood. 'I was into old cars and old tractors from a young age,' Mike tells me. 'When I left school, I went into contract machinery – things like silage cutting and working with diggers and I had a real interest in machinery.

'I began to realise, though, from a young age I had an eye for old stuff. It began, I think, with horse-drawn machinery and I was interested in restoring them. From there I began to get a few tractors and sometimes I would sell them. Really it was just something to do in the winter time, when contract work was slow. We had a workshop at home and there was always an old car being restored.'

Mike says he learned about collecting the hard way. Some items he lost on, others he made a few bob with, and each time he recycled the profits into other investments and acquisitions. In the early days he developed a passion for old Mini Coopers and began restoring and selling them. Any time he had a bit of money he would buy another one. 'I would always buy something old and after a time I moved it on again, and bought another one. That one item became two, and then that became four and then six and so on.'

The enemy of most collectors at some stage or another is space, as their interests begin to eat into the physical environment around them while they acquire more and more things. Luckily, or unluckily perhaps, Mike's father kept pigs at one time, and after he'd given them up there were a lot of empty sheds. 'I saw them as places to put things,' Mike says.

Through his work as a contractor he was in and out of farmers' yards and sheds a lot during his late teens and early adulthood. Where some saw a rusted old relic, good for nothing but to un-gap a ditch, Mike saw heritage and restoration potential. He picked up old horse carts and began to develop a lot of knowledge about these and early tractors. He would meet and seek out older farmers and pump them for information, asking them not only what machinery they used but what machinery their fathers and grandfathers used. It all happened organically, he says, and if you had told him when starting out that he would become obsessed with these things he wouldn't have believed it. He always kept his eyes open walking through farmers' yards and in his early twenties he began going to car boot sales and markets. By this time his interest had moved from tractors to tools.

'I began collecting a lot of small old items,' he says. 'I became fascinated, for example, with old ploughs and hand tools, and for a while I wanted to know and own every kind of tool the likes of the old thatcher and the shoemaker worked with. From there I collected watches as well, so bizarrely, I have a collection of them too. At one point, I then got into musical instruments and I ended up with a large collection of button accordions in particular. Don't ask me why.'

Aside from what he picked up around Munster, Mike also went to markets and fairs in the UK any time he was there on holiday or business. He remembers often coming home on the boat with the car boot stuffed full of old oil lamps or tools. In later years, he got involved in buying and selling property, but was often more engaged by the items left behind in the old farms and cottages he bought than he was by the house itself. There wasn't really any money in the collecting, but he did make money on items such as vintage cars, some of which he would acquire for clients and restore to order.

Every night, apart from scouring the ads online and in print for items to buy, he tracks values and tries to identify trends so that he might profit from buying or selling his stock.

'Once I got a computer, DoneDeal became part of my life,' he says. 'I was able to follow the market. Like if you go back 20 years, there might be value in an item and nobody five miles away would know about it. There would be things left inside sheds and no one was clued in enough to take photos of them and try to make money from them. The internet changed all that and people quickly began to realise there was a way of connecting items to buyers.'

Over the years, he has done well with several items, including a Model Y Ford car that had been owned by the same family in Rathkeale since the 1930s. When Mike came across it, following a bereavement in the family, it was covered in bags and dust. It turned out to be an original car and he brought it home and restored it. Even though he sold it five years later for a sizeable profit, he says looking back that he made a mistake and should have held on to it a while longer. But like many collectors, by that time his eye had moved on to other items and he needed to free up

Meeting a Man About a Hearse

some money. He came across the car recently for sale for a staggering amount of money.

Sometimes that happens, he says: he sees cars or items he sold turn up years later in all sorts of places. And sometimes the owners of items come looking for him. Two months ago, he got a call out of the blue from a man in west Cork, who said he thought he had traced his grandfather's tractor to Mike's farmyard.

'It was a 1940s tractor and he began to describe it to me and was wondering if I had it. He told me there was an unusual mark where a part of it had been welded, and I knew then I had it! I bought it 10 years ago for about €1,500, I think, and it had gone through about four or five collectors at that point. This man had traced its journey from collector to collector and eventually, he landed at my door.

'He came to look at it and wanted to buy it back for obvious reasons. I told him once I got the market value for it, I was happy, so we did a deal for about €5,000. I'm a bit reluctant to sell it, but because in fairness it has a lot of value for this man, I'll let it go to him. He was genuine and very nice about it.'

All this conversation has taken place in Mike's kitchen, during a lunch break from his day job, which is selling four-by-four jeeps in his family business a few miles up the road. He opens his laptop on the table and pulls up the ad for the hearse currently running.

The Personals

'The hearse for sale is out the back. I haven't had a lot of callers though. As someone said to me, there used to be fellas dying to get into them at one time,' Mike says. We're on the move away from the kitchen, and he leads me through a maze of outhouses and huge industrial-size sheds. We stop at a large shed at the back, having passed along the way the aforementioned wake scene with a life-size body in a bed and shawled figures kneeling over it. These items came from a building which was purpose built as a folk park some years ago, but had closed by the time Mike stumbled upon it. He had a look around and ended up buying most of the contents and so now has a wake and an old farmhouse scene set up in his shed as if it was a folk museum. Over the years, he and his wife have held set dancing and music nights here in the barn.

Just past these figures, in a corner behind gnarly machinery and boxes of tools, is a beautifully ornate, black horse-drawn Victorian hearse, complete with oil lamps and glass panels. It's the kind of thing you'd imagine the Krays would have been happy to be transported to their burials in.

It's in fairly good condition, but in need of some repairs here and there, and some of the glass panels have cracked. 'This is where the hearse has been lying for the last four or five years,' Mike tells me. 'It needs a little bit of restoration, but it's totally intact and

Meeting a Man About a Hearse

totally original. I don't really know when it was made, but looking at the old spoked wheels, and the iron bands on them, as well as the craftsmanship, I would imagine it is 150 years old.'

So this hearse, which dates back to some time around the mid to late nineteenth century – in a region which saw more than its fair share of death around then – has somehow been preserved and cared for, and ended up in this shed. How does someone come to have a hearse in the back of their shed in the first place? 'I'm not sure how to answer that one,' Mike says. 'It's like asking how does someone come to have a wife. Some things are just destined to happen ...' I'm pretty sure that's the first time I've ever heard someone compare their spouse to a nineteenth-century Victorian hearse. And they say romance is dead.

Has he any idea where the hearse came from? 'To the best of my knowledge it was somewhere around north Cork, Doneraile or somewhere like that,' Mike says. 'I know it was used until 70 or 80 years ago. I fell in love with it when I saw it. I've got a lot of calls about it. If I had a euro for every call, I could be on holidays full-time. A lot of the calls are curiosity and a lot of the calls are people that are undertakers that would like to have it as a showpiece. A few have come to see it.'

How much would he take for it? 'I thought it was worth about €3,000. I bought it with a collection.

The Personals

I think really somewhere around €2,000 would buy it,' says Mike.

Every week since he put the hearse up online a year or two ago, Mike has had enquiries about it, often from persons who are simply curious rather than serious buyers. In recent weeks though, he has had one genuine enquiry about the hearse, which may lead to a sale. 'An elderly man rang me from Carlow and said he wanted to buy the hearse,' he says. 'He had something like it one time, and was always looking for a replacement. He's due to come down next week to look at it, but if I had a euro for every time someone said that to me I'd be retired.'

What I'm trying to figure out is who really is going to buy it. I mean, it's not likely to be used for the school run. 'I would like to see somebody buy it who would look after it, and give it a bit of care and maybe restore it to its former glory,' Mike says. 'I would like to see it completely refurbished. But the most important thing is someone with the €2,000. After that we wish them good luck and hopefully they won't need it for personal use for a long time to come.'

Over the years, Mike says his wife has got used to him coming home with all sorts of artefacts and items. Perhaps she didn't bat an eyelid, but I have to ask what her reaction was when he arrived home one day with a horse-drawn nineteenth-century hearse? 'She reckons I should be inside it,' he replies.

Meeting a Man About a Hearse

Before most classifieds moved online, Mike trawled the print ads, but now he says he's a DoneDeal devotee and most nights, he checks through the ads for items of interest. 'I've been using DoneDeal for a while. It's a good way of advertising,' he says. 'Before that it was Buy and Sell. At night, when I finish work, it has replaced the television for me. I would be on it till 12 o'clock at night and I'm especially looking for something unusual,' he tells me.

What keeps him engaged is the fact that his range of interests is varied and eclectic. 'I also have a replica Model T truck, which I bought from a gentleman in Kilkenny and he hired it out to RTÉ for filmmaking. In fact, this particular truck was used in the making of the Michael Collins film. I sold a few very old tractors recently; there's a David Brown there in the middle of the shed, a 2D, which would be a very rare tractor, even though it doesn't look like a tractor. So, when I come across them, I just kind of pick them up and I like restoring them. Some people like to go to the pub. Other people do crosswords and different things. This is what I do, like. As my wife says, everybody goes mad in a different way. And when I come home from another purchase, she says, "Oh God no, do we really want another tractor?" She's very patient though.'

He's not sure what will happen to his collection after he dies. He has one son and from time to time he floats the idea of selling off the collection, especially as

The Personals

lately he hasn't had as much time as in previous years to take out the items and look at them. 'Maybe it would be easier if I only had one tractor and a small number of vintage tools,' he says. 'With the tractors, I have so many at this stage that I can't just take one of them out and drive it. I feel guilty if I do that and feel like I'm depriving the rest of them. The odd time for St Patrick's Day or local events they get a run out.'

He thinks there should be some incentive available to people like him who are committed to restoring old items – something like grant aid, for example. He looks at the next generation and believes that the passion and interest in preserving the older crafts and trades may not be there. The current generation don't see the same value in these things, he believes, and he's quick to point out he's not a professional collector in the sense that he's not looking to make money from his endeavours overall.

'You might think it's unusual I have gathered all this stuff,' he says. 'The collection of Model T Fords is probably my pension if I ever need to cash in. But to be honest, I don't ever see that happening. The day I stop adding to the collection is the day I stop living.'

PLOTTING A WAY OUT OF GRIEF

Mount Venus Cemetery plot with 3 graves. Current cost €6,000 but no longer required. Will sell for €4,500. *DoneDeal, October 2018*

It's not often you see death for sale. When I first saw this ad, I thought to myself surely there isn't a secondary market for graves and burial plots in Ireland? Wouldn't that just be typically Irish and in a way, sum up our obsession with land and property perfectly, so that even when preparing for death we are speculating and trying to make money from buying and selling land?

Then when I'd rung the seller and he'd told me he worked in banking, I had a thesis proposal and a *Sunday Business Post* column half-written in my head already. A few days after our phone call, at five past five on a soggy Wednesday evening, I found myself

The Personals

sitting at the counter of a traditional-looking bar in the affluent suburb of Ballsbridge in Dublin, ordering a Heineken zero (some craic I am) and waiting for a man selling a grave to show up.

The man's name is Richard, and he works in a bank nearby, and there's a party planned for a colleague in the back of the bar later so it suits him to meet here. He's in his fifties, and once drinks are ordered and brief pleasantries exchanged, he wants to get down to business and tell his story fairly swiftly. I'm surprised how quickly he wants to get into it, but later learn that he spent many a childhood holiday in Listowel, a town where if you threw a stone in any direction you were likely to hit a storyteller. So, wiping the froth from his upper lip, he leans in and begins his burial plot for sale backstory.

'Twenty-two years ago, my mother was told my father was very ill and so she needed to buy a grave in a hurry,' he says. 'She probably said she wanted to be buried beside him, so she needed two graves. The cemetery sold her two graves at £475 each, back in 1995, located up in Mount Venus Cemetery behind Rathfarnham.'

At the time Richard's father had been 76 years of age. His family had thought initially that he had had a heart attack, and so did his medical team, who even went so far as to fit a pacemaker and send him home. It wasn't until two weeks later that medics realised

Plotting a Way Out of Grief

that in fact he had a brain tumour. He became ill in February, and sadly by July, he was dead.

'The fact that he didn't have long to live was why my mother was anxious to buy two graves,' Richard explains. 'My mother was only 66 years old at the time. I accompanied her to the cemetery and we walked away with two pieces of paper that I now understand were folio numbers, or deeds, for the graves. So now let's move the story on two decades after that, to last year in fact, around the time of my mother's funeral. When we were making arrangements for her, we discovered that it wasn't actually two graves she'd bought, it was two plots; each of them was three graves deep. So we ended up with a spare plot.'

Some people lose the plot; it turned out that Richard and his family had found one. And instead of owning two graves as they thought they did, they now owned six. As the eldest in his family, Richard had the job of dealing with a lot of his mother's affairs after she died. Boxing away someone's life is an unenviable task. Personally, I've only had to help do it once when a close friend died. I remember thinking that it meant nothing to hired workers to throw a hoodie into a skip, but for me, that hoodie contained in its fabric the memories of a night out in Kinsale, or a walk along the estuary, or the day we both went to see the new *Rocky* film and put our hoods up like children. Inner lives are held in boxes in attics, forgotten loves locked away in torn letters, and there's both an intimacy and an invasion in going through someone's possessions after they've gone.

Unfortunately, someone's got to do it. 'I was tasked with doing the clean-out afterwards,' says Richard, 'and going through the paperwork and the contents, it feels awful because it feels like you're throwing out a person's life and the grief keeps coming up and grabbing you.'

There were boxes and boxes of letters to be sorted through. Richard tells me his father had been born in 1919 and many of his family had emigrated. Those were the days when people didn't phone or visit for long periods so letter writing was a vital link to home. His aunt, for example, went to the US in the early 1930s and didn't come home until 1958. Probably Ireland hadn't changed all that much in the intervening years. By way of illustrating this point, Richard tells me that every summer he went on holiday to Kerry and that there are seven years between him and his younger brother. 'My earliest memories are going down there in the early 1960s and that horses were still working the land,' Richard says. 'By the time my youngest brother came along he only ever saw tractors, because it had modernised so quickly. So there were huge leaps from then on that I don't think were there in earlier decades.'

Nothing he read in the letters gave him any greater insight into the lives of his parents though. Many were

Plotting a Way Out of Grief

formulaic and followed a very specific pattern. Most began with flowery language, describing how everyone was, what the weather was like, who had said Mass – that kind of thing. The next paragraph was generally all the news locally, such as marriages, deaths and other life events. And then the third paragraph was straight into the GAA football results and who should and shouldn't be playing in the local or county team.

'Clearing out the house of a loved one is a job far bigger than you think it is,' Richard says. 'All of a sudden you're hit with memories. The letters and the paperwork and the photographs are all triggers and you have to sit with those memories while you are clearing them away. So that all takes time. It was during this clearing out, though, that we discovered the deed for the two plots. None of us will need them in that area. As executor of the estate, it's my job to ensure everything has been divided up and the one thing left is the burial plot.'

Richard's first step was to offer the plot back to the cemetery. These days, a new plot goes for about €6,000, but they don't buy it back at that price. The explanation given was that they don't allow speculation on graves or plots. That's when Richard decided to put the plot on DoneDeal and see if anyone needed one in a hurry perhaps. When I met him, it had been up for two months and the ad had one more month to run. 'The only interesting thing that has come out of the ad is this conversation!' he tells me.

As we get a second drink, our conversation inevitably turns to grief. Richard has had three significant deaths in his life – his father's, his mother's and his younger brother's. I'm keen to find out how different the grief had been each time, or whether each death had been all that different from the previous one. 'My brother died of cancer and he was 36. He started getting a pain in his back and they all said it was related to a leg break he got while playing football. It went on for two years and then they found a lump and it was diagnosed as cancer. He had a cancerous node on his spine and that was causing the pain and it had a very high successful treatment rate of about 95–97 per cent.'

While the family were worried, they were given a lot of hope and optimism by his brother's initial diagnosis and the likely positive outcome after treatment. Richard's brother underwent treatment for six months, then had a reprieve – and then unfortunately, the cancer came back. His medical team wanted to do a bone marrow transplant and it had to come from a brother.

'My other brother and I did the test and we matched each other but not him,' says Richard. 'He was the odd one out. His chances went from 90 per cent to 70 per cent to 30 per cent to zero. He had two young kids, but he was very good-humoured despite all of what he had to endure. I asked him once, "Is there anything I can do for you?" He said: "If you can't get me a new body, there's nothing you can do for me!"'

Richard said his brother wasn't one to complain, which he thinks is partly why his cancer wasn't diagnosed a lot sooner. His brother remained good-humoured to the end, even telling cousins visiting him for the last time to have a great hooley at the funeral! That helped with the grief and when the end came it was relatively quick and his brother's suffering wasn't prolonged. He went to hospital on a Friday, on Saturday, the brothers had a robust exchange about how Gaelic football has changed over the decades, and on Sunday, he died. He had been able to drive to hospital himself, which is what he would have wanted.

Richard had been close to his brother – much closer than he had been to his father, who was almost like a throwback to the Victorian era. The grief of course is always much more acute when someone dies young. But he has ongoing contact with his brother's children, and that helps to keep the closeness.

We talk a little about retirement plans and Richard tells me he wants to give something back to the community and will get involved in some form of community education project after his time with the bank. 'I would aspire to trying to make a difference,' he tells me.

The Personals

We've finished our second drink and his colleagues have gathered and are giving him the nod that he must join them for a few drinks at the back of the bar. I tell him I've enjoyed our chat and that he's been an open interviewee and is a natural storyteller. He's pretty much resigned to not selling the plot at this stage, he says, but he's done his bit to take care of the last few loose ends after his mother's death. His duty fulfilled, his grief all but exhausted, he can move forward now with a clear conscience.

We shake hands and I say my goodbyes, but before I leave, he turns back and says something to me I don't quite understand. 'Thanks for letting me replay the tape,' he adds.

'What do you mean exactly?' I say.

'I think grief is like a tape that you replay over and over again until it wears itself out,' Richard says. 'So thanks for letting me play it one more time.'

Part Nine

SIGNS OF THE TIMES

NURSING HIDDEN DESIRES

Cross-dressing service. Hello!!! Genuinely and confidentially I have rendered my services for a long period of time so there's nothing to worry about. I provide my services in a beautiful, clean, safe, very discreet and a perfect and decent location. At your arrival, after a polite interaction in a conducive environment to develop trust and more friendship, you will be allowed to make your choices from any outfits of your desires in varieties. This includes *Material *Colour *Patterns *Sizes *Designs for any kind of clothes – lingerie, shoes and accessories and even fake breasts and hips you have ever dreamed to wear for complete elegance and perfect match. This will be kept safe for your personal use. If you are the type who is bold enough to go out for a girlie

The Personals

timeout with a dress sense that suits you, then I will gladly go out with you for a day or night to catch some fun, but if it's the other way round, don't worry, love, I am not leaving you out because you can also have loads of fun to experience indoors too. This ranges from *Having a bath *Face steaming *Cooking together *A glass of wine *Watching a movie together *Manicure and Pedicure *Interacting together in a full-time girlie chat and so much more ... Let me not forget the fact that I also make sales of shoes, clothes, lingerie and all accessories even jewellery – that's if you are interested. Trust me when I say this is my speciality and it's officially a place where you can just relax and be what you have always wanted to be (a beautiful classy girl). I also do a full make-up section and you will be so surprised with the changes and looks xxx
DoneDeal, September 2018

This ad is evidence of just how much the world of the personals and classified ads has changed since the move online. There isn't much that can't be bought or sold now, and the ads reflect this. Perhaps it's my

Nursing Hidden Desires

geographical bias, but when I think of cross-dressing services, Louth isn't the first area that comes to mind. If you pressed me, I'd probably say that New York, New Orleans or Notting Hill all come ahead of Louth in my imaginary cross-dressing league table.

Yet here I am on a bracing November morning, turning right out of Dundalk station, with Google Maps telling me that the bar I'm headed for is less than a 10-minute walk away. It's one of the few open at this time of the morning, and doing a brisk trade in full Irish breakfasts and freshly-baked scones. One of the bartenders kindly allows me to sit in a quieter as yet unopened corner of the lounge, and I settle in waiting for Tiffany to arrive.

I've asked for a quiet table, because to be totally honest, I have no idea what to expect, who I'm going to meet, or whether or not they will even turn up. When we messaged by phone days earlier, Tiffany seemed open to talking about the kind of service she offers, but she stressed she would have to keep some details confidential, which I expected. As I butter a steaming hot scone, I'm laughing to myself, because almost as if it had been set up, the music system is playing Whitney Houston's 'I'm Every Woman'! It's so loud that I have to ask would they mind turning it down a bit. Hello and welcome to your forties!

At two minutes past our appointed time, into the frame bounds a forty-something Afro-Caribbean woman with long curly hair and a beaming smile. I pour her tea and during our initial small talk she comes across as a warm and compelling advocate for her services. She is someone I could imagine wowing the investors on *Dragons' Den* some day as she rolls out her own brand of prosthetic breasts and killer heels for the modern cross-dresser.

I'm not expecting her to tell me that she's a trained nurse and came to Ireland to work in one of our hospitals. The cross-dressing service emerged quite casually from something she had been doing for friends, in which she would help them apply make-up or get ready for a night out. Sometimes male friends would ask her to apply make-up for them for a bit of fun.

'I began to realise that for some men though there is this strong desire inside them,' Tiffany says. 'It doesn't usually happen because they want to do it on a whim – it's because they are born with a strong feminine side, and they have this fantasy in their mind of feeling feminine outfits against their skin. So I noticed this among my group and people I hung out with and I thought to myself, why not see would there be a desire for a service to help men fulfil this side of themselves, outside of my group, if I advertise it?'

Taking the next step, Tiffany put some ads on a few sites online, and says she was taken aback by the level of interest. The service has become so busy in fact that she's even ditched the nursing career to focus on her cross-dressing business full-time! So how does it all work, I ask.

'I think you probably need to experience it to fully understand,' she says. I interject I'd be happy to try it, once she explains to my wife it is solely for research purposes. 'Don't worry about that,' she says. 'Some of the clients have their wives with them. Some wives are very understanding and you can interact with them. Some of course can't tell each other what they crave sexually or what they fantasise about. Their partners have this hidden secret inside them that they want to share with someone. In some cases, the wives will phone up and say their husband likes women's clothes and make-up and stuff like that and they want to book a session with me where they can come along if that's OK. Some of them are there to take photos of their husbands, and they look more like sisters when they are dressed up. For many of them, it is their fantasy and I have seen people of an older age, in their seventies, and this is what they have been dying to bring out of themselves for a long time.'

Before we get into the nuts and bolts of it, I articulate the fact that I find it incredible that someone who spent years studying for a nursing career, and moved halfway round the world to pursue it in Ireland, was able to leave it behind so soon and find such an unusual alternative, albeit one that is presumably more lucrative. Or is she just putting a positive spin on it for me?

'I know! It's almost hard to believe,' she says. 'But if we want to talk about the money, I have different packages. They vary from €250, which is the lowest package, to a top package of €2,500. The lowest €250 package has to do with make-up and an outfit. Then there is a €500 package and that includes make-up, five outfits, lots of wigs and different heels. There's one I have where you can go out to a club or pub or cinema. And then the €2,500 package has to do with unlimited outfits to choose from, overnight stay, any kind of lingerie you want, and I supply prosthetic boobs and fake ass.'

At this point – and maybe I'm being unfair here – but I'm imagining her meeting her grey-haired, golf-playing bank manager when she's looking for capital investment to scale up the business. And in case anyone gets the wrong idea, Tiffany is quick to dispel the suspicion that the service is a sexual one. It isn't, and the most clients can expect from her is a friendly hug. So more a cuddly than a happy ending then.

She gives me a rundown of the itinerary of the €2,500 overnight package. When clients arrive first she always starts with a nice chat and then they'll either cook something, or she will run a bath with lots of bubbles. From there she will offer different skin treatments that help relax the client's face and neck. She then helps to dress her clients in a fluffy pink dressing gown, which will be hanging in their specially-decorated pink bedroom. This is a room in her home decorated solely for the business. I suppose it's a good way to make use of the box room.

After she has moisturised her client's face, she can help them shave if they want and then it's on to make-up, manicures and a pedicure. She says all of this can be removed afterwards, so that when the client leaves there is no trace of the session and their femininity can once again be suppressed if they so wish.

'The transformation is just temporary,' she adds. 'It's a time when you can forget about everything in your life. And then when you go back home, you can be a man again and leave the women's clothes behind.'

After the make-up and manicure session is complete, clients choose a wig and pick from a large selection of outfits. Then she and the client and maybe some friends of hers will go for a night out, generally in Dublin, either to a club or the cinema. After that they come back and have a glass of wine together and watch a movie – more *Breakfast At Tiffany's* than *Predator*, I'm guessing. She says they will have 'girlie chats' and then get into nice pink pyjamas. Before bed, she will assist them to take off their make-up at their pink dressing table, and then the client will sleep in their pink bedroom.

She's selling a service which involves a lot of acting and role playing and fantasy, but also a huge amount of trust. She's such a warm and familiar person, I can see how someone who has long harboured a fantasy like this could be totally at ease in her presence. Until now, Tiffany has been remarkably open about the process and what it entails. It's only when I ask her what kind of people her clients are, where they work and would she mind giving me a sense of their backgrounds that she retreats a little.

'Jesus Christ, oh my dear, you would be so surprised to know who they are!' she says, tantalisingly. 'The most important people have this fantasy, people you would admire or know publicly have it. I have to keep it very confidential though. It is between me and my clients. But they are top people – married men, business people – it would really surprise you the kind of people who come for it.'

Never one to take no comment for an answer, I try to narrow it down by listing a range of professions, but Tiffany is not falling for it. She won't break under questioning. 'All I'll say is that it's not the kind of people you might expect,' she says, cryptically. 'Some of them told me this has been with them since they were children and they couldn't tell their parents, and then they held it from their wives. It's not a sickness or disease or anything like that, which some uneducated people will often say this is. From my experience, it is just something that people are born with and the part that's not normal is having to keep it secret and hidden from everyone, including those closest to them.

'So many of them tell me about when they were children and their parents left the house, and they went through their mum's wardrobe and their sister's wardrobe and tried to dress up and look in the mirror and feel OK with themselves. For some not telling anyone leads to problems in later life.'

There's a real sadness to all this, of course. Some of the men who come to Tiffany tell her it's the most relaxed and sexually liberated they've ever felt in their lives and also the most free. The feel of cotton or satin on their skin gives them inner peace when they're with her, and she has had clients who travel from all over Ireland to use the service. 'I do meet men who are trapped in a life that is not the one they want,' she says. 'Gender lines are so blurred these days. Some of the men will keep their collection of women's clothes at my house and have stuff they order online sent to me. They pay me a weekly charge to keep the items for them.'

I remark in jest that she's following the Ryanair model of add-on charges. 'It's all part of the service,' she says. Tiffany sees her role as part therapy, part fantasy enabler. Again, she repeats the point that I wouldn't believe the kind of people who want to play out this fantasy and that they are from all walks of life.

The Personals

While she may see herself as providing a therapeutic service, I mention that the men who come to her and don't tell their wives are surely on one level not being faithful? 'Coming to me, they know that it's never going to be physical,' she says. 'They know that and no matter what happens or how much they get to play out their fantasy, they have to leave my house and go back to their wife and family. Some can't talk to their wives; they feel afraid they will be judged and thought less of as a man and so I aid them with that. If I was to give any advice to married couples, especially new ones, it is that they should open up and not be afraid to be totally honest with each other.'

Essentially though, many of the clients are strangers who Tiffany invites into her home the first time she meets them in person. She says her safety is a big concern and she has some male and female friends who help her with the sessions. Sometimes clients don't want anyone else around and are very shy and she's happy to facilitate that, but only after she has thoroughly vetted them first. She says she provides the service safe in the knowledge that sex is never on the cards and that's made clear to her clients from the outset. 'There's no sex. I am very strict about that,' she says. 'It's just a place you can be a girl and relax. It doesn't have to do with any sexual intercourse whatsoever.'

As a former nurse, Tiffany thinks the seeds of her new profession were sown in hospital wards many years earlier. 'When I was working as a nurse, I met lots of patients and I am very outgoing and chatty,' she explains. 'I have a way of allowing people to tell me their secrets. I'm an open person and I can keep a secret even with a gun pointed to my head! I also have a lot of empathy.'

Tiffany loved nursing but when she moved to Ireland, the long hours meant she had little time for herself. She has always had more male than female friends, ever since she was a child, and has always been fascinated by make-up and fashion. So when one male friend asked if she would do his make-up, she didn't think it hugely out of the ordinary. And from there the business took off. In the four or five years since, it has become her main source of income and she says it is going from strength to strength. She's not the only one offering this service online I discovered when I did a search, but she does seem the most open and professional.

I'm curious to know whether her parents are supportive of what she does. 'I was a very honest child, so my parents know what I do,' she says. 'I relate to my mother a lot. I told her I do dress and make-up for men. I told them they just like it for fun and they come with their wives also. They support me. They know I am discreet and that my home is discreet also and they see me being happy, which is all they care about.'

When I ask Tiffany about her own life, she gives a loud infectious laugh. 'I am married to a man,' she says. 'An Irish man. My husband loves it. He supports me in everything, and he loves the fact I enjoy what I'm doing and he respects me for that.'

The bar we are in is filling up now and the little section we had to ourselves is busy with a group of elderly women in one corner and some men in hi-vis vests sitting in another. I've a train to catch, and she tells me she has a client coming later that afternoon so needs to prepare. We've spent maybe an hour and a half in each other's company and she's very easy to be around. Before we leave, I ask whether she ever puts her skills to use on her husband.

'It's not his thing,' she says. 'In general, there are some men who say they are a "man's man" and you'll often hear that. I think, though, a real man is not afraid of that side of them, but some I have met are afraid of their partners and of the reaction of their family.'

As we're walking out, she tells me that having done this for several years now, she believes that some people are destined to never be sexually content in their lives. 'They end up with depression,' she says. 'They are so happy when they are with me. It changes them. They become vibrant and you can almost see the anxiety and worry disappear. You can see lines going away on their faces with each touch of the make-up brush against their skin.'

CUT-PRICE COUNSELLING

Relationship advice for a low cost. If you have experienced abuse in past or present relationships, I would like to offer insight, advice and a friendly outlet to anyone who has or who may still be suffering. I have an understanding of behavioural psychology and the dynamics of an abusive relationship, and so am keen to use my experience to help others. I want to offer my services more as a workshop than an actual job, and so I would accept donations of €10 per hour in order to get things up and running. If you want advice, or even just someone to listen, I am more than happy to hear you. *DoneDeal, January 2019*

The Personals

I'm not sure what kind of person I had in mind as the poster of this advert. It's a pretty unusual one, buried in the Other Services section of DoneDeal, which I glance at from time to time to find items that don't quite fit anywhere else. Possibly I was thinking that Joan was someone in her late forties; maybe she had been through some difficult personal experiences, and along the way she'd done an evening course in counselling and wanted to gain some practical experience and a few bob.

The ad was curious also because it's a not-for-profit enterprise. There are hints that the person behind it has experienced some of the issues they expect to deal with. So after a couple of failed attempts and rescheduled meetings, one unusually mild January morning, I found myself sitting in the back corner of a Costa Coffee cafe in a suburb of Cork, waiting for the would-be counsellor.

I'm a bit taken back when a young, waif-like woman with long dark hair and chocolate brown eyes walks in. She's wearing a leopard print coat, and there's a hint of Amy Winehouse glamour about her. She bounds over to my corner table with a burst of energy and mischief. Apart from her appearance, the first thing I notice is that she has an incredibly strong Cork accent, and she apologises in advance for the amount of cursing she says she's likely to do during our chat. She doesn't drink coffee – it makes her too hyper, she

Cut-Price Counselling

says – and so has tea instead. She is an absolute bundle of energy so I cannot imagine what a hyper version would be like.

Once the formalities are over we get straight down to the reasons she placed the ad. 'I have been in difficult relationships and I have friends who have also,' she tells me. 'For most counselling sessions, it's €70 an hour. If I had €70 to spend on myself for counselling it would have saved me a lot of hassle. But like most people, I couldn't afford that. And then apart from the money, when they go for counselling sometimes people get told all sorts, like they can't have an addiction before going into relationship counselling and so on. There's a lot of reasons why you have an addiction and often many of them are because of what you are going through. So, both are interlinked and I want to make it easier and more affordable for people to get help.'

Joan is the kind of person all her friends turn to when they have an issue. She's not qualified as a counsellor, although she has taken courses in psychology and social work, but she feels she offers a shoulder to cry on. The idea of the service she's now offering is that people with problems can contact her and she will offer sound, non-judgemental advice over the phone and then, if the recipient should feel like giving her money, she will accept a donation for her time.

Even though she's barely into her thirties, she has met so many people who are traumatised as a result of

The Personals

relationships. The common thread with many of them is that they don't know what they want from partners, and they keep going into new relationships and repeating the same mistakes over and over again. They never press 'reset' and that's where she comes in.

'A lot of women I know over 30 still pick stupid men,' she says, bluntly. 'I would love to educate men, and women, on what is right and what is not. People have a concept of love. Most don't have a fucking clue what it is. They say, "Oh I love him" and yet he could be kicking the shit out of them. That's not love, it's not even close.'

During the hour or so we spend together she talks at a hectic pace, jumping from subject to subject, landing on sentences like a cat toying with a mouse. She is refreshingly honest – and idealistic perhaps in terms of placing the ad and hoping for the kind of responses she expected. But she's not naive. Far from it. For the first 20 minutes that we're chatting she riffs on relationships, and when she's not speaking from experience, she's telling me about choices friends have made.

'To me love is being in a relationship and you don't have to worry about it, and you don't have to worry about not trusting him either,' she says. 'You're not thinking about their temper, and you can bring them out and they won't cause a scene. Love is knowing they care about you, knowing that they will make you laugh and that they are good for your mental health. That's love.'

On nights out she spends a lot of time observing the people in her group getting drunk, when underlying aspects of their personalities that are not always attractive really come to the fore. She doesn't drink, but has more positive opinions on smoking weed.

'I'm a loud person and I take in a lot of people's behaviour. I watch why people behave the way they do. I don't drink.' She later speaks about her belief that smoking weed benefits some people's lives. Not only does she believe that it helps some people function in certain social situations, but she's also convinced it helps to overcome the trauma of past relationships. Putting on my rehab hat, I suggest that it must be just like any other addiction in terms of its impact. 'Can you control addiction? No. But can you manage addiction so that it's not completely fucking your life up? Yes.'

Maybe she's got it figured out, but I'm not so sure. Fifteen years ago, when I was in rehab, I heard addicts (myself included) make all sorts of deals with themselves. Some alcoholics I knew convinced themselves that white wine with dinner didn't constitute drinking alcohol! Many would tell me afterwards that smoking weed was not relapsing, despite the fact that whatever way you look at it, you are putting a mind-altering substance into your body.

The Personals

I was so paranoid about relapsing after coming out of treatment that I don't think I took a Nurofen or a Disprin tablet for about five years afterwards, for fear it might lead me back down the road to chaos again. So Joan believes that it is better to be addicted to some substances than others? Well, maybe that's just the addicted mind making all sorts of deals with itself in order to remain in active addiction. Or maybe it's true and we need to get away from the all-or-nothing view of rehab and living. Although the Catholic temperance society the Knights of Father Mathew tried mass abstinence programmes in the nineteenth century, they didn't really have a lasting impact.

I'd often heard Joan's argument made about so-called softer drugs. Over the years many people who have had alcohol problems have tried to convince me that smoking weed following treatment for alcohol addiction wasn't an issue. I've no doubt that some went on to live less chaotic lives and managed to balance their relationships far better than before. For others, smoking a joint every other day eventually led back to the chaos and substance addictions they had previously escaped from.

I express my reservations about controlling any substance once you are an addict to my new counselling friend. She's not buying it for one second. 'Stoners are not the same as alcoholics,' she tells me firmly. 'Completely different drugs. It might be the same underlying reasons why they're using it, but the outcome is different. Listen, dude, people won't be losing their family over smoking weed, like. Some people are losing the plot before and that is nothing to do with addiction – it is often to do with a relationship. Smoke helps them not lose it.'

She says that she can understand why people remain in abusive relationships for long periods of time after what she has seen around her and the courses she has studied. 'I know people in their twenties and they go through a lot of mental and physical abuse in relationships. Many do that and then swear never again,' she says. 'Sometimes it's almost funny. You know when people don't get what they want? They get all nice, then they get angry, and then all nice again and then angry. It is really funny to watch it; it's like a circle.'

When you analyse this cycle closely, as she has done, she says it's all to do with control. 'At 16 or 17, when you meet your first real fella, if that is a bad one, it sets the tone, like, and you think, well, that's what a relationship should be,' she says. 'I just think people need to be educated more and that's partly why I want to reach out to others.'

Joan put the advert online just a few weeks before I met her. She asks for a nominal €10 payment, and feels that if she could have spoken to someone for less than €10 per session years ago, she would have done much better sooner. The idea came from wanting to

The Personals

help others avoid the mistakes she has made and to try and unravel a little more about herself through hearing from and interacting with others and their struggles. The responses so far have mainly been from men, which is not what she hoped when she posted the ad.

'There was just one genuine guy who rang me and I was delighted as he was telling me about his sister and asking for advice. But in general, I think men got the wrong idea about the ad. Maybe they thought I was going to find someone for them? I had a man ringing me at all hours of the night – like, at four in the morning – so that wasn't what I wanted.'

None of the men who contacted her forwarded any donations, and she was very disappointed with the responses. She thinks maybe she needs to rethink where to place the ad online, and while she would still like to help people, she's a bit more wary now. I pose as a potential customer, and ask what advice she would give someone who phones and says they're in a destructive relationship.

'I'd ask them why can't they get out of it?' she says, 'And then I'd tease out what brought them into it in the first place. When people come to me, I ask them if they can see any resemblance between the person they are with now and the person they were with on day one. Usually the answer is no.'

Sound, solid advice, I tell her. Why, though, if she is so keen to help others – and I've no doubt how genuine her intentions are – doesn't she train to be a professional counsellor and make it her career?

'In the future, I would love to go to school,' she says. 'The thing is though I have a learning difficulty. I can't put words on paper like other people can and I would have to pay €500 to get assessed again. I don't have that money. There were nice thoughts that went into the ad and I did think men and women would benefit and that I could help. But really, I wasn't prepared for how many creepy men would ring me though. I think men over a certain age think of the internet and just think sex. Every man was asking me was I with someone.'

The ad may have to be taken down and she'll try to think of another route. In fact, as often happens with some of the more off-piste ads, I had been the first proper contact she'd made. She's rethinking her strategy and has reality TV in her sights as inspiration. Naturally.

'If people are dealing with abuse or they just want to come for relationship advice, how to find a nice guy or what guy would suit me, then I'm their woman to talk to. Although, I sometimes think maybe I should think of something different. Do you ever watch *Million Dollar Matchmaker*? I would love to set that up over here.'

Aside from her professional ambitions, these days she is years away from the difficult break-ups of her

The Personals

past and is in a good place relationship-wise. 'I'm with a lovely person now,' she says. 'I pick my best friends as partners now. A lot of the men I was with weren't always loved by my friends. I didn't want to be hanging around with my fellas all the time or bringing them to places with my friends. With this guy now though, he is like my best friend. I can take him anywhere. He is trained! He is respectful and he loves me for who I am. I am loud and feisty and some men want to change that. Men get intimidated by me. My boyfriend is the most secure person in himself. He's not paranoid. He's not doubting himself all the time. That's a key difference in that he doesn't project whatever insecurities he may have on to other people. I know from experience if you're with someone who is paranoid, essentially you're with two people.'

And while her fella sounds like a mix between Prince William and George Clooney, she says she will be slow to marry or have a child with him, despite the fact that he's very much in favour of it. 'I don't believe in divorce and I think people get married just for a ring now,' she says. 'My fella said our taxes would be lower – that nearly swung it for me! I would like to have kids but it frightens me. I am traumatised still. I would get healthier and fitter if I was pregnant. I'd never do it for myself but I'd do it for my kids.'

Trauma takes many forms. For some it can be a slow burn, while for others it can be a short yet sharp impact. Sitting across from me in the cafe is someone clearly dealing with ongoing and unresolved trauma, but who has managed remarkably well to continue being an employee, a partner and a forward thinker, despite the odds being stacked the other way. She knows deep down that she would love to have children. She knows too that her partner would be a great father. But she also knows that she cannot allow her trust to be breached again, and so she is living life in a controlled way, denying herself certain things in order to keep the demons and the unpredictable thoughts at bay. Or, as she explained in her wonderfully blunt way: 'I said to him: "If we get married and have a kid, what if you become a total prick?" That happens to a lot of fellas.'

She says her nerves are not good and if, for example, the baby had colic, or was a poor sleeper, she's not sure she would be able to cope. We talk about fitness and its benefits for positive mental health, and she tells me that because she is naturally thin, she is worried that too much exercise would make her too skinny. I force a 'Yeah, I hate that' smile, patting my middle-aged paunch, and pushing a half-eaten muffin away from me as if I'd never intended to devour it.

Arising from this casual conversation comes one final fact about her life. I ask if her thin body type is a genetic trait in her family? 'Nah, I'm adopted,' she says. 'I met my birth mom once, when I was 21. I'm actually from Romania. The only way I would describe it is it's like that place Borat is from in Kazakhstan – that's exactly like where I'm from. It's weird. When I was there I was looking around and they didn't speak English and I had a translator and she wasn't great. She wouldn't say half the stuff I was asking my mother, like why did she have me adopted, why didn't she keep me?'

She tells me that the meeting with her birth mother was fraught and not the fairy-tale reunion she had imagined as a child. The first thing she remembers her birth mother saying when they met was asking whether she could come back to Ireland with her. This obviously startled her and made the encounter tense.

She had had a pretty good idea about the circumstances of her adoption prior to meeting her birth mother. She knew, for example, that she was adopted at the age of two from an orphanage in Romania, along with two other children. While they all did well, she says they all had their unique difficulties to overcome, such as behavioural and psychological issues. Her background is complicated by the fact that her birth parents live apart and in very different circumstances.

'My mom lives in a hut and my dad lives in a mansion,' she says. 'When I met her, she kind of hugged me but it was really weird. The story I'm told is that my dad moved away and took some of my siblings and I was left and they couldn't afford to take care of me. I know my mother had nowhere to go and my uncles couldn't keep me. I don't blame her. I am glad though. My adoptive parents here were lovely. I love my mom and dad. As my dad said, there are lots of puppies in the kennels and they decided to choose one of them instead of making a new one! They were amazing people and made me the person I am today. And that's why I really want to help other people.'

Now I understand why she wants to reach out to others. Many of her peer group are not aware of her background or ethnicity. She says it's not that big a deal, and that her impressive command of Cork slang coupled with her strong accent means it never really comes up in conversation. She's fixed and comfortable with her identity, rooted as she is in the People's Republic. Sometimes though, when she's in the city and she and her friends see other members of the Roma community, one of the group might mutter something about them, something racist. I tell her this must be really difficult for her – knowing that those closest to her are unknowingly criticising her heritage and identity.

Not for the first time, she responds in her unique way: 'Nah, boy, doesn't bother me. I say to them, "Shut the fuck up, would ya? That could be my aunt!"'

THE HOMELESS HOTEL

Looking for 2 plus bed property for homeless HAP €1,912. Hi, I am on homeless housing assistance payment (HAP), with a rate of €1,912 per month. I am a single mother with 2 children aged 4 and 5. We are in emergency homeless accommodation up the north side and spend 2 hours each day commuting to south side schools. I am also a full-time Masters student in UCD. I would be very grateful if there are any landlords renting in south Dublin or even the Bray area who would consider renting their apartment or house to me. The council will pay a deposit and one month rent up front, as well as a reliable and assured monthly payment, among other benefits. I can move in whenever and do not care if it is furnished or unfurnished, just looking for somewhere to live. *Gumtree, January 2019*

The Homeless Hotel

It's 6.50 a.m. on a bitterly cold January morning, and I'm on a 100-metre walk with two children aged four and five and their mother. She's a single parent in her early thirties, and she resents the icy air this early in the day because her youngest child has been coughing for the best part of a week, and was especially sick during the previous night. Every 30 seconds or so, the child had been consumed by a fit of coughing and as a result, the family had broken sleep all night. Coupled with this, the medication her daughter is taking is making her itch a lot. At least, she hopes that's what it is. There's always the concern when you're not in your own bed as to who may have slept in it before you, or what may be lurking under the well-worn mattress.

If this family were in their own home, they'd have it properly investigated and perhaps as a precaution get a new mattress and ditch the old one. But that's not an option for them. The family lives in a hotel room: two small beds, one desk, one television, one mini-fridge, one kettle, one hairdryer. Two children and one adult. More often than not, they sleep in one bed in that room, so if one of them is sick, they all share that sickness and suffer. If one of them doesn't sleep, none of them sleeps.

From this cluttered hotel room, where homework is done on mattresses and takeaway food is heated up in a microwave and made to last two days, they travel for almost two hours across the city to reach their school

The Personals

and crèche. Shamefully, they are one of hundreds of families in Dublin city who are being housed in hotels and B&Bs in Ireland in 2019, as the housing and homelessness crisis intensifies and shows little sign of abating.

Someone said to me in a recent interview that when you cut through the spin about Ireland's 'recovery', our problems only became apparent when we began to house homeless people in hotels and tourists in homes. And there's some truth in that. Almost two years before I met this family, the Minister for Housing, Planning, Community and Local Government, Simon Coveney, made a commitment in March 2017 that no family would have to live long-term in a hotel room. Despite this, and some initial improvement in the statistics, the numbers are once again on the rise.

Back in the car park, once both children are belted in, we begin the journey from this hotel masquerading as a home on the north side of the city. Mary feels guilt every time she catches sight of her half-asleep children in the rear-view mirror. They should still be in bed, and yet here they are, without breakfast, being whizzed across the city, their normal childhoods flashing past as fast as the oncoming buses. Most mornings they drive first to her parents' house, near where they used to live in their own home. This was before their landlord decided he could get more money from 'professionals' and told them they had to leave because he was selling the house. The for sale sign never went up and some weeks later, Mary saw the house re-advertised for an even more inflated monthly rent. This had been her home – it had been commodified and traded as if it were a sack of rice.

Mary says she registered a complaint when she realised what was going on, but now thinks it doesn't matter; she's out of there and all her efforts now are focused on trying to get her family out of a hotel room and into a home. Every day she trawls the ads online looking for a property that falls within her budget of close to €2,000 a month. That's €500 a week for two bedrooms for her and her two children. She says she can't even get viewings, and that although landlords and agents are prohibited from profiling prospective tenants in receipt of social welfare payments, somehow they have ways of finding out. She says that initially many estate agents are enthusiastic, but the vast majority never call her back for a viewing.

She became so desperate that she decided to post the above ad. It had been online for four weeks when I phoned her. Unfortunately, she's had no serious offers, except for one person who has put their house up for sale and said she could rent it until the sale went through. 'To be honest, I put the ad up and forgot all about it until you rang,' she says. 'Because I qualify for a HAP payment, I think they just filter me out.'

Her allowance comes to €1,912 a month and she is prepared to pay €100–200 a month in cash on top of that, even though she's not working and is in full-time education. She knows of many families in her situation who are handing over illegal cash payments up front to secure houses, even though they are on very limited incomes. Such is the competition for housing at present that she cannot get emergency accommodation on the south side of the city, even though that's where her children go to school and all her family live. She's also studying for a Masters degree in law on the south side.

Not only is she on a waiting list for social housing, as are tens of thousands of others, but she now finds herself on a waiting list for 'family hub' emergency accommodation. This is a waiting list to get on a waiting list for a home. The hotel she is in at present has a separate entrance for homeless families and individuals, on the side away from the regular entrance which paying guests use. While there is a kitchen available to families and a small playroom, she says this has to be shared with homeless families and individuals on six floors. She estimates that there are up to 70 homeless people in this part of the hotel.

While she's there, she keeps to herself. She doesn't like her children playing in the communal areas or cooking with other families. Partly this is out of shame and embarrassment, but she's also very protective of her children and doesn't want their situation to become normalised through engaging with others. As a result, it has been almost six months since she cooked her children a meal. This makes her feel inadequate as a parent and serves as a daily reminder that she's not providing for her children as she feels she should be. I tell her the opposite is in fact the case, that she is clearly going to extraordinary lengths to do what she can for her children. Deep down she knows this, but the disruption of being homeless is clearly impacting on her sense of wellbeing.

By 7.45 a.m. we arrive at her parents' house, where she and her kids will finally have breakfast, nearly two hours after they'd all woken up in their cramped room. The support of her family has kept her sane, she tells me, and allows her to cling to some semblance of normal life. She's not hopeful that she will get a council home any time soon, given that she's been five years on the waiting list. Others she knows have spent up to 15 years waiting.

Once she and the children have had breakfast, her second commute from her parents' house to the school and crèche begins. This is a much shorter journey and everyone is in better form and more alert when I join them along the way.

Just after 9 a.m., once she has kissed her elder child goodbye at the school gate, we sit in her car. When I ask about the impact of living in a hotel on her kids, she becomes emotional. We sit for a few minutes while she dabs at the tears on her cheeks with a Starbucks napkin. 'It's had a huge impact,' she says. 'I'm getting my son psychologically assessed because he is not coping well at all. Aside from the upheaval of this, I think he may have Asperger's. He has an appointment tomorrow. I suppose this does hit me hard because, would you believe it, I went through the same thing myself with my parents. We were homeless for four years when I was younger.'

The tragedy of inter-generational homelessness for this family underlines how poorly housing needs have been addressed since the 1980s and how cyclical our housing problems have become. There's almost a fatalism about it. The same fatalism often struck me when, for example, former Mountjoy Governor John Lonergan commented that he knew the parents and grandparents of prisoners in his care from their time in jail. Is it a stretch to say that these days some social welfare and housing officers are experiencing the same cycle, having dealt with and tried to house the parents of the young mothers and fathers who are trying to access their services today?

'We were a family who had come back from the UK and when I was a child, from the ages of nine to 12, I was homeless,' Mary explains. 'This for me is like history repeating. I do think I absorbed a lot of stress when I was younger, and this time around I find it harder because it is impacting on my own kids and I know how it will leave a lasting impression. They should have their own room, maybe a garden, and the security of knowing where they will be next week. They don't have that and I feel huge guilt because of it.'

She and her children found themselves in a hotel after her relationship with the father of the children broke down. Initially, she moved back in with her parents, but there were 11 people living in a three-bedroomed terraced house and pretty soon tensions began to rise. She says she had to leave there before things got out of hand, and that because she left voluntarily and declared herself homeless, she feels she's not a priority for the council. That's why many question the official homeless figures. There is a whole community of hidden homeless, squeezed into box rooms in their parents' mid-terraced, three-bed homes, or couch-surfing with friends or moving between numerous properties. The most public manifestations of homelessness that we see – usually rough sleepers – are just the tip of the iceberg.

Mary's ultimate plan is to become a solicitor, but the pressure of studying full-time, balancing parenthood and not having a home is clearly having a negative impact on her studies. It's a vicious circle, she says, and she feels that the system is stacked against someone like her moving into employment and away from dependence on social welfare and housing assistance payments.

The other factors she has to cope with are unnecessarily long days. Often, she doesn't get home with the kids until 7 p.m. By this time, they'll have fallen asleep in the car en route, and she has to wake them to walk the 100 or so metres from the car park, through the side entrance and upstairs to their room. They then go straight to bed. There's no chance to unwind or relax or have quality family time.

The rules in the hotel mean that she's not allowed any guests who are not approved in advance. Generally, families are also not permitted in each other's rooms. She's not allowed to walk around the corridors in pyjamas, and the children are often prevented from playing in corridors or play areas. The people she shares the floor with come from all kinds of backgrounds and range in age from teenage single mothers to elderly single men and women. In her class at university only one other person knows about her personal circumstances. She is afraid too that the father of her children will find out she is homeless and blame her for not being a good enough mother. I try to reassure her that any fair-minded person would say that she is doing all she can in very trying circumstances. It's not her fault that she is one of 10,000 homeless people let down by society's failure to invest in adequate numbers of social and affordable homes.

One of the hardest things for Mary is that she has been given no indication of when she will have a front-door key. She simply wants a place to call her own, and where her children can experience a normal child-

The Homeless Hotel

hood. Hope is a scarce commodity when you're living in a hotel room hours away from all support. The situation gets to her at times, but because every day is such a struggle, she tries not to overthink but to live in the now, however difficult that may be. She will leave the ad up for another few weeks, but doesn't have much faith that anyone will respond positively.

'I'm just a statistic,' she tells me, before departing for her college class. 'I try not to think about the future as it can be overwhelming, so I just try to take one day at a time and focus on other things. It's the only way I know how to get through it.'

MAKING STUDY PAY

Leaving Cert notes – 590 points! I achieved 590 points in my Leaving Certificate in 2016. I am selling my notes that I compiled to help me achieve these top grades of A1. The price of €20 per subject is a small price to pay as one grind is €35 avg. covering a chapter whereas these notes cover the entire course. Please text me with any queries you may have, also please leave a contact number if emailing me so I can reply. ***DoneDeal, January 2019***

Niamh McGrath is one of those children your mother or father compared you to unfavourably as a child when you weren't applying yourself fully. With a wagging finger and deliberately enuciating each word as they barged into your room early on a Sunday morning, they might have said: *'You don't see Niamh*

Making Study Pay

McGrath out all hours of the day or night a month before her Leaving Cert do you?' or '*Do you think Niamh McGrath is at home pestering her parents to be allowed go to a rap concert?*' You get the idea. You grew up resenting the Niamh McGraths of this world, not because of anything personal, but because of how others held them up as shining examples of golden children, to be cited in instances when you disappointed a grown-up.

Sitting across from me in the foyer of the Kingsley Hotel is a confident second-year pharmacy student at University College Cork, who readily admits that for her, school and studying came naturally and was something she embraced wholeheartedly. 'I wasn't that good at sport,' Niamh tells me, between mouthfuls of sparkling water, 'so school for me was something I was natural at and I loved school and everything about it.'

Niamh's mother works as an accounts clerk and her father is an engineer, and looking back, she says that both pushed her academically. They supported her love of science and maths from a young age. 'If I ever struggled with science my dad would always guide me,' she says. 'He would have stressed the importance of education. We'd get killed if we had bad grades!'

Anyone who has sat the examination knows about the intensity of the Leaving Cert year and the huge pressure and stress it places on students. Even for a natural student like Niamh, it was an attritional experience in which every hour she had was accounted for and studying became her sole focus. She stopped playing camogie in her final year so she could squeeze every last minute out of her timetable and downtime to study. She told herself it was just one year and that the 100 per cent commitment and focus would be worth it.

Her typical weekly schedule involved after-school study from Monday to Thursday from 4–6 p.m. This was when she got her homework done. She then went home, had some dinner and was back at her desk at 7 p.m. and studied until 10 or 11 p.m. on a normal night. In the weeks immediately before the Leaving Cert, this study session could stretch into the small hours of the morning, while on Saturdays she attended supervised study for most of the day.

Coupled with this, Niamh had weekly private grinds in Irish oral work. She was lucky that her next-door neighbour was a retired Irish teacher and an advocate of the language and working with him gave her a shot at a high grade. From an early stage in secondary school she'd had her sights set on pharmacy. For this she needed just short of 500 points, or at least three A1s and a few high B1s or A2s. In the end, she got four A1s, including one in honours maths. When she compares her extraordinary results with those of her contemporaries, her success in science subjects and maths bucked the trend of the grades achieved by other girls she knew at the time. She feels this is the result of a lack of confidence in tackling the subjects, due in part to negative social conditioning, which is belatedly being challenged.

'You do still get that narrative that women will go towards what I might call the more feminine careers, such as teaching and nursing,' she says. 'And the current statistics will show that boys are better at more maths- and science-type subjects, while girls would tend to be more natural at English and languages. That's the general experience anyway.'

I was surprised, in an era where gender equality is positively asserted and every family probably has two parents working, to hear Niamh tell me that certain careers are still being suggested predominantly to one gender over the other. 'I remember a big push for nursing in school for all the girls, and definitely I don't remember boys being encouraged to do nursing to the same extent,' she explains. 'Hopefully, though, that's changing.'

When she totted up all her grades, Niamh got 590 points in her Leaving Cert so had a bit to spare to get on to her course. The final year when she put in long hours and late nights paid off, but rather than being glad it's all over, she finds university life very different in comparison. She really liked school, she liked getting homework and she liked the assistance of and interaction with teachers along the way.

The Personals

'I enjoyed the help of teachers but now in university, you could never bother to turn up if you didn't want to. No one would say anything. It's all down to yourself. I moved out of home, and am getting used to having everything on my shoulders.'

Pharmacy is one of the toughest courses she could have chosen. It involves very long hours, so much so that she finds in the evenings she has little energy to study. It's the kind of course where students need 100 per cent attention and focus in lectures to be able to process the sheer volume of information given to them on a daily basis. It's made all the harder, she feels, because despite her success in the Leaving Cert, she doesn't believe it adequately prepared her for university study.

'It was all about learning stuff off and regurgitating it,' she explains. 'In the first year in college you're still in that mindset, thinking that what you study is what will come up in exams. But it's totally different and they are likely to throw anything at you. The only point of the Leaving Cert really is to motivate students to want something and work hard for it. I know parents won't thank me for this but a lot of what you learn is never used again and the main skills you get are stamina. It doesn't prepare you at all for the next phase of life though.'

Niamh found other ways to make her Leaving Cert results pay dividends. A few years ago, she remembers seeing an interview with a student who got seven A1s. He had received some of the highest results in the country and he said in the interview that he planned to sell copies of his study notes online. She remembers thinking it would be great to get her hands on the notes; that they might just give her an edge. She became obsessive about notes during her Leaving Cert preparation, and assembled carefully catalogued folders for each subject.

'I remember after the Leaving Cert, thinking it was such a shame all the work I had put into these will be just locked away. And then I began to wonder would someone be willing to pay for my notes given all the effort I had put in?'

And so Niamh put her study notes for four of her subjects – the ones she got A1s in – up on DoneDeal, charging €20 for each subject. She says this compares to about €35, which someone is likely to pay for a private grind.

When I meet her, it's been two years since the ad has been up and initially, she tells me, she was completely taken aback by the response. 'I expected a few calls at the time, but was not prepared for the volume of interest,' she says. 'It blew up. And every year since, especially around the time of the mocks or the Leaving Cert itself, I make dozens of sales. I am making a steady €7–800 a year from it and I have the notes in email form now so I just forward a copy each

The Personals

time. It's a nice little earner coming up to Christmas or Rag Week for me.'

Mostly, Niamh doesn't have to deal with follow-up queries, and only a handful of buyers have demanded she send the notes as hard copy. She stopped doing this as it was costing her too much to produce and to post them.

The buyers all seemed satisfied with what they got. Take her Irish notes, for example; she will send complete essays which can be learned off by heart or tailored to fit topics. All her notes go beyond what a student would get in the classroom from their teacher and she has curated various courses and approaches which she has used. The notes are such a hit that several teachers have also bought them from her! One of them was writing a maths book and asked if he could incorporate some of her material, while she's also had panicked calls from parents doing everything they can to get their young Jimmy or Mary over the line with weeks or days to go.

Niamh doesn't see herself leaving Ireland after her degree is complete. She's too much of a home bird. If she was Minister for Education for a day, she would alter the curriculum to make subjects more relevant to potential careers. 'I think subjects should be more relevant to industry. I also think that career guidance needs an overhaul and that's no reflection on any of the wonderful career guidance teachers I had. In

Making Study Pay

general, it needs to be less gender specific. One of the girls I live with qualified as a nurse, and she hates nursing but it was what was strongly encouraged for her. She would have been a brilliant engineer, for example.'

Despite some narrow gender stereotyping that still exists, we discuss how much has changed in recent decades when it comes to women's opportunities after secondary school. Practically all her female classmates went on to third level almost automatically. She says that is some pivot in a generation. 'My mother did not go to third level. In her time, it was more a case of what job are you going to get when you finish school? Now, women are focused on their careers, as well as being wives and mothers. In my course, for example, 70 per cent of the students are female. It's fantastic to see that.'

Her tip for parents who may have children studying for the Leaving Cert is to be there as a support but not to push their kids too much. On reflection, she reckons the times her father was nagging her to study were her least productive times, when almost as an act of rebellion she wouldn't make as much effort. I tell her I'm not convinced by this and that if my own mother hadn't frogmarched me to my room and plugged out the ghetto blaster, then I'd likely still be repeating the Leaving Cert to this day.

On the flipside, the more a student can take ownership of their own results and work on their own

The Personals

initiative, the easier it makes the transition to the next level. But not every parent has a child like Niamh – an incredibly driven 22-year-old who adored school and homework and study, and continues to reap the rewards, both personally and financially, of all those long hours of study and sacrifice. As a parent, all I can do is sigh!

ACKNOWLEDGEMENTS

After our second child was born I disappeared most nights from 7 p.m. till the early hours writing this book, and without the love and support of my wife and family, this obviously wouldn't be possible. So, a big thank you to my wonderful wife Sophie and to Óran, Luke and Eva.

As a child, my mother took me to the local library in Ennis every week without fail, and I want to thank both my parents for all their help and support over the years when my career choices seemed, well, a little off-kilter. Aoife, Sinead and Damien have been a great support as well as Tom, Tayto (I always call him Damien) and Lorraine and their families.

To my fantastic agent Faith O'Grady, who kept belief in this project, a huge thank you. We discussed it several times over the years, honing it and developing it to a point where it could be presented to publishers.

To the really great team at HarperCollins, including publishing director Eoin McHugh who shared my

The Personals

vision for this book from the very beginning and helped shape and better it all the way along, as well as George, Patricia, Tony, Nora, Jennifer, Micaela and everyone who worked on it and brought it to life.

The genesis for this book began with a series of reports I've been doing on RTÉ Radio1 over several years. I am very grateful to all on the *Today with Sean O'Rourke Show* team for all their help and support getting those reports to air. In particular, thanks to series producer Tara Campbell, who always found space for these reports, to presenter Sean O'Rourke for rolling with them on air so well and to my colleagues Geraldine, Deirdre, Cora, Alastair, Fiona, Mary, Paddy, Evelyn and all on the TodaySOR and RTÉ Radio1 team. You can listen back to some of those reports by going to the RTÉ Radio1 website.

When I was in secondary school in Rice College in Ennis, English teacher Mannix Berry had a significant influence on my later direction in life. At a time when teachers in general were concerned with rote learning and points chasing, he imparted a love of English and critical thinking and I remain forever indebted to him for that.

There's a wider group of readers, friends and colleagues who have given me valuable advice and support and cynicism (!) along the way with this book. Thanks then to Ella McSweeney, Shane Hegarty, Nick Kennedy, Edel O'Connell, Aidan Mulcahy, Ray

Acknowledgements

Scannell, all the Blarney Boys, the Golden Girls, my long-time friends Eilish Hughes and Mark Anderson, Michelle Timoney, Miriam Donohoe, Liam O'Brien, Evelyn O'Rourke, the Cavanaghs in the US, wonderful neighbours in Ard Dara, the ever-supportive Madeleine Johnston and Charles Olden, Chloe and Shane, Therese (for putting up with me, she says), Eoin Ryan, Niall MacMonagle, Maurice Gubbins and Craig Hughes. I know I've forgotten people, but there have been so many who helped with this book I couldn't possibly list them all.

I lost a very good friend, musician Brian Carey, in 2017, and he was always one of the first to read or listen to my work over the years. I missed his feedback during the writing of this book and I'll miss him for lots of other reasons long after it hits the shelves. This is for him, and for Fia.